RETURN TO YOUR ROOT

Also by Rav Dror Moshe Cassouto
UNLOCKING YOUR TRUE POTENTIAL
THE BOOK OF THE WORLDS
IT'S TOO MUCH FOR YOU

for children
THE TALE OF THE RABBI AND HIS ONLY SON
THE PRINCE MADE OF GEMSTONES
A MIRACULOUS TALE

RETURN TO YOUR ROOT

◆ ◆ ◆

A Guide to Reincarnation,
Soul Actualization,
and the Complete Redemption

◆ ◆ ◆

Rav Dror Moshe Cassouto

Emunah Project Inc.

Copyright © 2022 Dror Moshe Cassouto

All rights reserved.

Emunah Project Inc. is a 501(c)3 non-profit organization dedicated to producing and disseminating faith based media to the entire world.

For more information, visit www.emunah.com

For all inquires including orders,
email info@emunah.com

FIRST EDITION

לעילוי נשמת

L'iluy Nishmat
David Leroy Arner

Dedicated to His Memory
and Eternal Benefit

Brad Arner

Dedicated to my wife and five beautiful boys, my friends, followers, and everyone who has helped and supported the Emunah Project. Special thanks to Shalev Powers, Pinchas Shwartz, Esther Fink and everyone who helped make this book possible.

Contents

	Introduction...i
ONE	Methods of Soul Transfer..............................1
TWO	Transfer of Character Traits & Personality.......9
THREE	Finding Yourself..15
FOUR	The True Path..21
FIVE	The Final Redemption...................................41
SIX	Redemption & The Secret of Repentance.......55

ADDITIONAL
INFORMATION

    Procreation and The Soul................................63

    The Sparks of Our Souls..................................64

    God is With Us..66

    The Sin of Adam and Eve................................69

    The Nature of Our Reality...............................71

    The "Backend" of Creation..............................78

    Spiritual DNA...87

LECTURES & TEACHINGS

Judgments of the Heavenly Court..................93

Who Am I?..102

The Importance of Holiness and Purity.........104

How to Understand The Creator..................110

Miracles in Our Days..................................112

How to Face Impossible Situations...............114

"Oh God, Create Within Me a Pure Heart"....117

A Conversation with The Creator.................121

Having Faith in our Positive Influence..........123

Why Your Prayers Aren't Being Answered.....125

The True Nature of The Creator...................130

Time, Space, and the Final Redemption........135

The Redemption Will Come Through the Internet..140

The Mission of the Final Redemption...........144

ABOUT THE AUTHOR..............................147

INTRODUCTION

A Blueprint:
How to Return to Your Spiritual Root And Help Usher In The Final Redemption

Who Are You?

It's a deep question, but most people probably won't take it that way. They'll give you answers like "I'm an accountant." "I'm a doctor." "I'm a stay-at-home mom." Some will simply tell you their names. While there is nothing wrong with such answers, they only scratch the surface of a much deeper truth. There are deeper truths about who you are to be realized, deeper truths to be found.

Souls Are "Transferred" From One Generation to the Next

In this book you'll learn in detail about how souls are incarnated to the world, how they are composed, and how they are "transferred" from one generation to the next, and why it matters.

This complex process is commonly called "reincarnation" in English. There are two main types of transfers that take place, and they are the "soul-rope" and *ibur*. There are also other methods of spiritual influence that souls effect and are affected by, namely "sparks" and the "transfer of character traits and personalities." The explanation of these concepts in the beginning chapters will lead us to the deep teachings that follow and conclude the book.

What's the Spiritual Meaning of *Tshuvah*?

In contemporary times, *tshuvah* is used in the religious sense to mean someone who repents and either comes back to observe Judaism after staying during a period of time, or someone who grew up irreligious, but returns to the holy path Torah observance of their ancestors. Both "repentance" and "returning" are definitions of the Hebrew word *tshuvah*. It also means "answer" and is used to define the answer given to a question asked to a rabbi, often of the topics of Jewish Law or textual study.

"Returning", "repentance", and "answer" are all proper definitions of *tshuvah,* and one can understand how their overall concepts are similar. Hebrew words often are defined in other languages using several different words, also conceptually similar but whose definitions are different. For this reason, even the most well intentioned translations of the Hebrew Bible and other sacred texts can never yield the depth and multiple meanings of the verses that can be found by one who knows how to study them in Hebrew..

Rebbe Nachman's holy book *Lekutei Moharan* quotes the Holy Zohar's explanation of *tshuvah* as "returning to the place of one's (spiritual) origin." Literally, "coming back to where one was taken." This is speaking about the spiritual place the soul originates in the upper worlds.

Each of our souls is unique and comes from a unique place within a higher Divine structure. According to the Zohar's words, one who completes their *tshuvah* is one who reconnects to the place of his spiritual origin during the course of their life. It can be understood as "finding yourself" in the deepest and truest sense of this overused and cliche phrase.

In this book you'll learn how to find yourself truly, how to know yourself in a deeper way, and how to develop an understanding about your soul. This is taught in the first part of the book, which focuses on the internal understanding, the inner/spiritual aspect of this process of returning to your root. The second part is the fulfillment of these inner/spiritual understanding, which culminates in action in the physical world. In short, it's not enough to *know* who you really are, you must *be* who the Creator made you to be.

What Is Required for a Return to One's Spiritual Roots?

Mere learning cannot move one to his true place; physical action is required for a complete return to one's spiritual root.

All this information is fascinating and extremely practical for the spiritual truth-seeking individual, but the scope of this book is geared toward an even higher purpose. The purpose of this book is to pass every individual seeker a key of information and a design or blueprint to help humanity in the much bigger picture. This will be discussed in the final chapter.

Return to Your True Self, and Aid in the Redemption of Humanity

By the end of this book, with help from Heaven, you will understand the importance of returning to your true self, how to actualize it, and how the Redemption of humanity is tied to this important concept of returning to one's spiritual root.

CHAPTER ONE

Methods of Soul Transfer

Part One
THE SOUL ROPE

Parents Pass on Parts of Their Souls to Their Child(ren).

The main aspect of our soul is that which we receive from our parents. This is the main life-force and vitality that carries us through life. It can be described as a "rope" that hangs above the head of every person. When a man has an intimate relationship with his wife or soul mate and they conceive a child, part of his rope passes to the child and unites with the feminine aspect of the soul of his wife, forming the soul-rope of their child. The soul of the child is literally a combination of their mother and father's souls. When that child grows and finds a soul-mate, the child they have is a combination of their two souls. It is through this structure, that all souls are made, and also are connected through an expansive family tree that encompasses all humanity.

The Soul's Inner Vitality and the Un-Corrected Soul

There is another aspect to this transfer of soul which can be described as the inner vitality of the soul rope. The substance of this soul-rope is this inner vitality of the soul, which is the spiritual energy or substance that makes up every soul. Through every generation, a portion of the soul's vitality is divided up and channeled to all of its descendants. You might imagine a giant tree of sorts, with many branches, that connects children to their parents, and their parents' parents, for many generations all the way back to Adam and Eve.

Because only a small portion of the soul's vitality is passed to their children, every consecutive branch of this "tree" decreases in size, This is the hidden spiritual level of the Rabbinic dictum "the decline of the generations," as every soul of the consecutive generates are smaller and smaller in stature of their spiritual vitality.

For example, Adam, the first man, had a certain portion of soul that was given to him by God. For our purposes, let's quantify this portion that he was created with as 100 percent of his soul.

Each of the children that he had, received a portion of his original soul.

The portions of Adam's soul that reached their correction stayed with him and ascended to Heaven when he passed from this world. However, the portions of his soul that still needed correction after his sins, were transferred to his children in varying amounts. Therefore, Cain, Abel, and eventually Seth did not all receive equal amounts of Adam's original 100 percent of soul; they only received the portions of their father's soul that he was unable to correct. Let's say that they only received 10 to 15 percent each of his original soul.

Souls Are Connected Throughout all Generations

The parts of the soul they received from their father were still gigantic, because his original soul was so massive. These 10-to-15-percent portions of Adam's soul were transferred through the generations in the same method described above, up until the current generation of souls. Again, by envisioning a giant tree with Adam and Eve as the massive trunk and their descendants as the first offshoots, one can understand how our souls came to exist today.

One can also imagine the greatness of the souls of the earlier generations and our small stature in comparison to theirs. If Adam only passed a small percentage of his soul to his children, and his children, in turn, passed only a small portion of their vitality to their children, the effects of the continuation of this process for many generations. Avraham our forefather was already 20 generations later than Adam. And it's been thousands of years since he walked the earth. Our souls contain tiny fractions compared to the vitality as the souls in the ancient generations.

Describing the "decline of the generations," the Talmud records: *"R. Zera said in Raba bar Zimuna's name: If the earlier [scholars] were sons of angels, we are sons of men; and if the earlier [scholars] were sons of men, we are like donkeys."* He was speaking about only several generations ago, and already commented on their inferiority compared to their recent ancestors. One can only imagine the difference between us in our current time compared to our ancestors and heroes of the Bible and sages of earlier generations.

The differences in vitality between one generation and the next is very pronounced and *is* as drastic as it sounds. We're like specs compared to the vitality of our ancient ancestors, but this is the understanding of vitality in one aspect. But from another perspective we have the same DNA as them, so even though our spiritual stature is very small we come from the same "stock" as them and are, in spiritual essence, exactly as they were. Just in ancient times, they had much more vitality building their souls.

Via this structure of soul-ropes, the inner essence of the soul, the soul's vitality, and the parts of the uncorrected soul, are transferred and connect all souls throughout all generations. The soul-rope is the main essence and comprises the main part of a person's soul. The other types of soul-transfers and spiritual influences on the person's soul are described in the following parts and chapters.

Part Two
IBUR: THE 2ND TYPE OF SOUL TRANSFER

Helping Souls With Their Mission on Earth

The second type of soul transfer we will discuss is known in the writings of the kabbalists as *Ibur*. In Hebrew, Ibur means "impregnation" or "incubation."

Ibur happens when a soul receives Divine help in the form of another soul that comes down from Heaven and unites with them. This soul that comes down assists their host for a certain time period to help them with a particular reason or mission.

For example, the Ramchal, Rabbi Moshe Chaim Luzzato, was connected through Ibur to two holy righteous souls that assisted him with his holy work. These souls joined inside him with the soul he received from his parents. The two souls were those of Moses and Rabbi Chaim Vital (who was the main student of the Holy Arizal). They are hinted at in his two names, Moshe Chaim (Luzzato).

The Soul of Messiah - Leading Holy Souls to Redemption

Mashiach (the Messiah) will also have souls of righteous ones attached to him. The main souls he will carry will be the souls of King David and Moses. *Mashiach's* role will be to help those souls finish their complete correction. Although these holy souls achieved vast heights in this world, no soul has ever reached their absolute completion. Absolute completion of even the holiest souls throughout history will only happen on redemption day.

Because of *Mashiach's* great power, he will be able to correct the greatest souls through the generations. By the merit of *Mashiach's* effort and struggle, the souls of King David, Moses, and all those who await total completion will achieve it.

As all souls reach their completion, the entire world will be shifted; and the redemption will take place.

Part Three
SPARKS: THE 3RD TYPE OF SOUL TRANSFER

Sparks of Soul in the Physical World

The third soul transfer method occurs when "sparks" gathered within the physical world build the soul. The sparks in creation merge with our souls when they are consumed, used, or interacted with.

For example, when a person eats fruit, the soul sparks contained in the fruit merge with the soul of the consumer, and some of the sparks are incorporated into that person's soul. In other situations, other sparks that are corrected are *not* merged with the person's soul, because their correction was completed through other means.

These sparks are trapped within all of creation. Through our interaction with them using our five senses (not just consumption), these sparks may be released from their entrapment in the physical world.

For example, there's a story of the Arizal, where he was walking with his students, and he stopped and kicked a certain rock. He explained that there was a soul stuck in the rock that was waiting for him to release it for 500 years.

In a similar light, there is a story about the righteous man Rebbe Yahuda Zev Lebovitch when he was young. As a child, he walked with his father, the saintly Rabbi Yechiel Tzi, in their town in Hungary. He saw souls trapped in the trees and needed help, and he told this to his father. His father told his young son not to worry about them for now but that he would help them one day.

Everything in Creation contains an inner Spark within it. Through interactions with them, these sparks reach their destiny. Such interactions can include eating food or using inanimate objects, and many more. Sometimes these Sparks' destiny is to join onto our souls like in the example of the fruit mentioned above, but sometimes not. Like the spark of fire flickers away, sometimes the Spark reaches its completion simply by being used and is not added to our souls.

These relationships describe the inner and spiritual system that is the inner workings of the physical world. Everything in this world has an inner essence, and the spiritual relationships that happen are reflected in the physical world.

For example, let's take the example of a family's dining room table. There is a spiritual essence to the table, a spiritual Spark clothed in the physical world by the wood, screws, and varnish that comprise the table. As the family uses the table for their meals, Shabbat meals, holidays, and events, spiritual combinations occur.

As they sit at the table, their souls interact with the Spark of the table in a spiritual dimension. Once the Spark of the table finishes its purpose and destiny, the table won't be used anymore. And it will either break and be thrown away or replaced and discarded. The physical events that happen will be an outward manifestation of what takes place in the inner spiritual dimension.

The example of the dining room table illustrates a general description of the types of spiritual relationships that are the foundation of our world.

Also, learning Torah is a way that sparks and holiness join onto the person. The Torah has unlimited Sparks, and this is a secret spiritual meaning of the well-known dictum that the Torah is infinite.

As long as a spark has existence, its physical counterpart also exists. Once the Spark is used, the object finds its way to be destroyed in one way or another. Examples of this are plates breaking, furniture being thrown away, fires consuming houses, etc.

This process can be understood as a transfer of energy from use to disuse. It's like an inner, spiritual "song" of everything in Creation. Every Spark has its story and then reaches its destiny.

Part Four
THE FOUNDATIONAL SOUL OF
EVERY GENERATION

Moses: *Adam HaShalem* (the Complete Man)
– His Soul Close to Perfection

The main core of the souls of Adam and Eve is passed through the generations via the soul rope of the holiest and purest people of each generation. Often, these are well known leaders of the generations whose writings and commentary we still enjoy today. They were in all generations, including the days of the judges, prophets, the Great Assembly, the *Mishna*, Talmud, and up to and including our days. This great soul of every generation is the *tzadik yes olam* (righteous pillar of the world).

The main component of Adam's soul was present in the soul of Moses, King David, and every main soul of the generation. King David received all of his soul from Adam directly, and not from his father's original soul. This is because Adam wanted *Mashiach*, the Messiah, to arrive; therefore, he gave the most unique and beautiful light of his own soul to Jesse, King David's father, who passed it directly to King David.

Moses himself received the soul of Adam and brought it close to perfection—closer than any other person could bring it. This is why Moses is called *Adam HaShalem,* the "Complete Man." This is Moses.

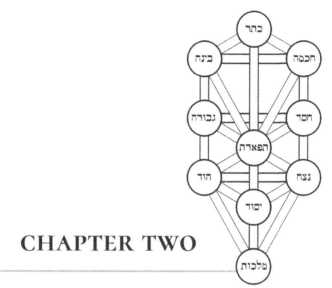

CHAPTER TWO
Transfer of Character Traits and Personality

Part One
LARGE SOULS

Holy and Unholy Traits Passed on for Generations

"Everything is connected" is a common spiritualist saying.

As Jews, we've known this truth since ancient times. When we say, "Hear, Oh Israel..." we remind ourselves of the unity of the Creator and His intimate connection with every detail of creation.

This world is "connected" with itself not only in a general sense but also within a super-specific system, a vast web of cause and effect that spans time, space, and all borders of physicality.

Who Are the Large Souls? The Heroes From the Bible

This type of "Large Soul" transfer is in contrast with that described in Chapter 1. While the soul rope transfer method is rooted in physicality (soul transfer from parents to child), this type of soul transfer of character and personality is not bound to ancestry or lineage.

The following are some examples:

Going back through history, especially ancient times like those described in the Bible, we see that the world was occupied by "Large" Souls. These Large Souls were great in their spiritual roots. The portions of the soul they received from Adam, the first man, were especially important and distinguished.

We're of course talking about all the heroes from the Bible such as Noah, Avraham, Isaac, and Jacob our forefathers, Moses our teacher, King David, and many more.

However, these Large Souls were not only born within the family of Israel. The Zohar teaches that the soul of Pharaoh, King of Egypt, was ancient and powerful. The Talmud recounts the great rulers of Rome were the descendants of Esau, the son of Isaac. Great sages of the last generation thought the offspring of the nation of Amalek were responsible for the horrors that were wrought on the Jews in Europe at the hands of the Nazis, may their names be obliterated.

As we see, "Large Souls" doesn't necessarily mean "holy souls."

The aforementioned web of cause and effect starts with these Large Souls and their actions on earth. Depending on what they did on earth, their personalities, attributes, and deeds create an effect on future generations. These things are transferred not only to their direct descendants but also to their spiritual descendants, the people who receive portions of the Large Soul essence.

Abraham, our Forefather, the Embodiment of Kindness

His Kindness Was Passed Onto Future Generations

For example, let's think about our forefather Avraham. He was the embodiment of kindness. Many stories teach about his hospitality and the great effort he took to teach about faith in the one God to everyone he could. After he passed away from his body, his huge essence of kindness was passed to people throughout future generations. Someone who lives in our current days and who feels a deep passion towards kindness possesses a spark of the light of kindness of Avraham our forefather.

While our forefather Avraham was the embodiment of kindness, he certainly had other character traits and tendencies as well. Because he was such a central soul in the history of creation, his other traits and tendencies were also passed down to generations of souls after him.

Whatever these Large Souls do during their lives carries an effect on the souls that follow them, whether for the good or not.

Moses' Anger

This Anger Entered the Hearts of People in Later Generations

Moses, our greatest leader, experienced and acted on anger, as recorded in the Torah itself. The anger that found its way into the hearts of people generations after Moses can be rooted in his mistakes of anger.

This cause and effect can be drawn even from the most basic physical tendencies. For example, Tziporah, the wife of Moses, may have tended to bite her lip during the years of her life. Think about everything that happened in her days. She certainly had no shortage of stress and pressure! This simple action from such a Large Soul could create spiritual waves that carried through time. Today, there could be thousands of women in the world who contain within themselves an aspect of Tziporah, the wife of Moses, and bite their lips in times of stress and uncertainty in the exact way she did.

The examples can go on and on, but the main idea is that the transferal of the character traits and elements of personality from these earlier Large Souls have significant effects on the generations until this day.

Part Two
EMOTIONS - HABIT - ACTION - THOUGHT - AND SPEECH

Traits Are Transferred to Generations by the Souls of the Past

Character traits, emotions, habits, actions, thoughts, and speech patterns of the Large Souls of the past transferred in some way to the souls of history that followed them. But it is not only large souls who can have an effect. Also, people of less renown and stature can cause an effect, but their impact would be less than those of the main heroes and ancient characters.

In metaphorical terms, a small stone cast into a pond has small ripples, but a large stone has much greater ripples; a giant boulder would send water on the pond's banks! Giant souls are the "boulders" who affect many generations and whose even small actions can have generational effects.

Character traits and personality are the main connection that connects later generations to earlier ones but names, talents, occupations, and geographical locations can also be points of connection.

For example, if a certain righteous man in the times of the Talmud experienced an event that caused him great sadness, that sadness could manifest into the lives of those who connect to his spiritual root in some way. Names and professions can also hint at connections between souls.

Love of Torah - Passion to Serve The Creator

This Was Passed to the Hearts of Later Generations

Most clearly, the love of the Torah, as well as the passion and desire to serve the Creator that was fostered in the hearts of the righteous ones of the past, make it into the hearts of those who serve the Creator in the later generations.

This vast web connects us to the Souls of our past, yet it's also important to remember their true root: Adam, the first man.

CHAPTER THREE

Finding Yourself

The Large Souls Performed a Majority of the "Work" of Soul Correction

Yet, They Have Not Fulfilled the Mission Here, We Come in

We've now discussed the multiple ways that souls transfer through the generations: the rope method, Ibur, sparks found within creation, and finally the web of cause and effect. Through the lens of these fantastic revelations, let's try to understand how it all comes together in an individual of this generation.

The souls of this generation are very small compared to the vitality of the ancient souls found in the Bible and even later times. For example, the *Amoraim*, the sages whose discussions are written in the Talmud, praised the lofty status and greatness of the souls of the previous generation, the *Tannaim*, the sages of the *Mishna*. The *Amoraim* praised the greatness of the *Tannaim's* greatness and extreme superiority to their own and admitted their relative weakness and lowliness. But they were only several generations apart!

Today, almost two thousand years later, we can only imagine the lowliness of our stature compared to theirs, let alone to that of the prophets, judges, and our forefathers, who compose the entire foundation of the Nation of Israel.

There is no doubt that we are very far removed in stature from the ancient Large Souls. In reality, we are like the thinnest branches on the top of a giant tree, connected to the Large Souls by generations of previous branches whose offshoots have sprouted successively thinner and thinner through each succeeding generation.

Our Souls Are Smaller in Stature Than our Ancestors'

Our souls are smaller in stature than our ancestors' because we are at the "peak of the pyramid." That is to say, their souls were so much greater than ours because they were dealing with much more of the original vitality of Adam the first man. As each generation continued, they corrected a great part of their souls. Whatever they weren't able to correct were passed onto the next generation. So, each succeeding generation has inherited a smaller amount of soul.

In that aspect of vitality, we are smaller in stature, but in another aspect, we have a special quality that even they did not possess. The truth is that they were the ones that performed a majority of the "work" of soul Correction. They have already fixed most of what was needed, but they have not completed the mission. This is where we come in.

We Have the Role of Fixing What They Weren't Able To

In This Way, We Are Very Great

It's our job to correct the final pieces of soul that slipped through the cracks and remain, awaiting their completion. In many ways, what we are charged with is fixing the hardest things of them all, because what was "easier" was already within the grasp of earlier generations to fix. We are left with the rest. Here we stand, smaller in stature, the smallest branches at the end of the tree, the small capstone of giant pyramids, yet we are responsible for accomplishing what they were unable to. In this way, we are very great.

Our main vitality, of course, comes from our parents by the rope transfer. *Ibur* from righteous people joins our souls even today. We also gain the sparks that are found in creation, and are affected in large part by the web of cause and effect.

Surely each one of us would admit to ourselves that we can be complicated. We each contain a depth of personality, character, likes, dislikes, and so on. While our environment and the events we experienced through life certainly helped influence who we are today, we may also be aware of deep personality traits that we have had since we can remember. One person may be naturally compassionate and empathetic to the people they come in contact with, while another person may be more focused within themselves and not as sensitive to the world around them. One person may be drawn naturally to give charity, while another person holds a passion and desire to seek out and expose injustice.

The reality is, every one of us is a mixture of many tendencies across a vast spectrum of emotions, habits, and desires. Some people are simpler than others. Some people are carrying heavy burdens of admixtures of varying and sometimes extreme tendencies, such that they may be diagnosed with mental illness by today's psychologists.

The Root of All our Tendencies Is Spiritual

The reason that we are the way we are is often the result of sparks of the Large Souls that found their way into our being.

As explained, a person who experiences anger could have received those sparks from the anger of Moses himself. Now, just because the said anger was from Moses, doesn't mean it's acceptable to be angry. Moses had reasons to be angry, but it doesn't mean that it was okay. The Torah itself testifies this anger was the reason Moses our Holy Teacher did not merit to enter into the Holy Land.

Practically, if someone holds within themselves anger or any other trait that in itself is not proper, even though an argument could be made to its validity, their behavior may not be excused.

Take the example of the person who inherited Moses' anger. Perhaps the Creator arranged for them to receive this anger so that they would be able to rectify this trait within themselves, and thereby fix a part of Moses' mistake. The lesson is that no matter what, we must always accept upon ourselves to fix, balance, control, and straighten our character traits.

As another example, consider a person who is very prone to depression when they look at the spiritual state of Israel and the rest of the world. So much is happening to our families and friends' families that children, God forbid, are falling away from the path of Torah. Immorality is normalized through pop culture and powerful secular organization. This person is overwhelmed by what they see and often experiences great depression. For the sake of this example, let's say that this trait of sadness was inherited from one of the righteous men who witnessed the destruction of the Holy Temple in Jerusalem. He experienced such extreme bitterness by witnessing the falling of Israel's Temple and spiritual stature that this spark of sadness passed through generations and made its way into the heart of this person who lives in our days.

Now, just because this person is sad because of a "noble"

reason doesn't mean it's okay to be sunken and low in depression. The Holy Rebbe Nachman of Breslov teaches that depression of any sort is extremely damaging spiritually, and should be avoided at all costs. Therefore, even though this person's sadness originated from a righteous man in the ancient days, they still must work on the flaw.

We as Individuals Can Be a Mix-and-Match of Aspects and Influences From our History

Appreciate and Understand the Depth of Who We Are

The point illustrated by the two examples above is of course that no matter who a person is or the nature of their flaws, they should take it upon themselves to fix their negative habits, thoughts, emotions, and on.

Now we can understand in a general way how we as individuals can be a mix-and-match of aspects and influences from throughout history. But can we know exactly which aspects of which individuals we possess? Generally, these specific details are hidden from us and are numbered among the Creator's secrets. They remain hidden from everyone but the highly dedicated spiritual seekers, who can see specific details about themselves or others by the means of spiritual visions and other means that hold a fragment of prophecy. But it's important to know that these wondrous phenomena are only bestowed upon the person by Heaven, and are never granted through means of force by the individual looking to achieve such things.

The general realization we should settle upon is to simply appreciate and understand the depth of who we are and how we are composed of such ancient roots, and likewise understand our place in this grand picture. We are the ones who the Creator intended to fix the "peak of the pyramid", the final portion of the structure of the souls of the generations.

CHAPTER FOUR

The True Path

From Learning to Action

Merge Your Soul Perfectly With Your Earthly Experience.

The main purpose of all learning is to transform it into action. How does one materialize the deep lessons in the previous chapters into action? The answer lies within this chapter.

This chapter contains the most precious advice from the whole book. The main purpose of all of these wonderful teachings is for you, the individual, to learn about yourself and become who you're meant to be. This is the secret of repentance.

As described in the introduction, repentance means to return to your spiritual root. Your spiritual root is the "place" where your soul originates in heaven. Completing your repentance is to fully realize who you are as a soul and merge it perfectly with your earthly experience. This is the true purpose of your life. Simply put, to be who you were meant to be.

To achieve this potential, there is a two-step process. The first step is spiritual (inner), and the second is "physical" (outer). First, we will explain how one works at accomplishing the spiritual aspect of repentance. Then we will discuss the materialization of the spiritual work.

Step One
RETURN TO YOUR SPIRITUAL ROOT

An Overview

The first step of the repentance process is to connect to who you are at the root of your soul. Through the examples of the types of soul transfers in the previous chapters, you should now have a deeper understanding of the structure through which souls are incarnated and interact in the world. Try to get to know yourself. Think about your parents and your family tree. They are the main vitality of your soul that extends and connects back to the Large and Godly Souls of Adam the first man and his wife Eve.

Also remember there are many souls of righteous ones who are interacting with the souls of our generation through *Ibur* — helping us, guiding us, fixing spiritual flaws within us, and assisting us in our spiritual efforts.

Soul sparks that are contained within food, drinks, and more merge with the individual and bring them both closer to spiritual completion. This is happening within people around the world, each possessing a "piece of the puzzle," and together (whether aware or not) we are completing the entire creation.

Find Out Who You Are

The main aspect of the first step of repentance is to search within yourself and find who you are. Honest self observation will lead you to find your unique qualities and character. These inner qualities are the main roots of your soul. To know them means to know and understand yourself.

Look back at the examples found in Chapter 4 and apply them to your own life and yourself. You should get to know yourself more openly by realizing your soul's natural character and tendencies.

Some people are naturally kind, others are shy. Some like to use their mind to think about deep issues and try to solve them, others consider this mentally exhausting and rather focus on other things. Some are fascinated by the mechanics of the human body and enjoy learning about health and exercise, while others are inspired by completely different topics.

Such differences can go on and on. Recognizing your qualities is the essence of the first step of repentance.

When a person pays attention to their natural positive inclinations, interests, emotions, and habits, they are connecting to the main roots of their souls that stem from the lives of the righteous ones of the past and originally from Adam, the first man.

Self-Acceptance

Accept Yourself & Dedicating Effort to Self-Control and Improvement

In looking within, it's important to accept yourself, without judging yourself negatively, the way you are. For example, one person may have been clenching their fist for as long as they remember. Ever since they were a child, they have clenched their fist all the time.

Why should they judge themselves for this? They shouldn't. Perhaps this habit comes to them from the root of the soul of a righteous man who also clenched his fist. We shouldn't judge ourselves for being the way we are. Life is very deep and meaningful, and so are we ourselves.

Even a person who is always angry and frustrated shouldn't blame themselves for being the way they are. What if this person's anger comes from the root of the anger of Moses or King David?

However, this lack of self blame and judgment shouldn't be confused with the complacency of not taking responsibility to improve and fix within ourselves what should be fixed.

The ideal approach is to not feel bad about ourselves for being how we are and at the same time dedicating effort to self-control and improvement. As explained earlier, this improvement corrects the flaws in the roots of the soul, which connects back to the righteous ones. Fixing ourselves causes much deeper spiritual roots to be fixed that are hidden from our awareness.

Once a person feels more connected to who they are in their spiritual roots, it's time to take on the second step of repentance. The second step is the most fantastic and freeing experience and completes the purpose of our existence.

Step Two
YOUR PHYSICAL WORLD: TAKE ACTION

An Overview

Once a person connects to their main roots of their souls, it's time to actualize them in the physical world. This process can be described as taking the inner conclusions of self-awareness and putting them into action in everyday life.

This fulfillment of your soul's pure desires and tendencies can come in the form of careers, hobbies, side jobs, and more.

Using the conclusions you found on your inner path, make your best effort to choose a path in the physical world that best aligns with who you are.

Surely, we all have heard of inspired business owners, chefs, craftsmen, or the like who proclaim they "were born to do this." This is exactly what we're talking about — finding what you were "born to do" — because you truly were born to do something (or several things).

These conclusions are not always very clear to every person. That's why the first step of self-realization and getting to know who you are is so important. When you know yourself, the path to fulfilling the destiny of your soul becomes clearer. You know what you need to do; you feel it.

Follow Your Soul's Inner Roots

Have Faith in its True Importance

There are some people whose passion can inspire them to start a business in a certain field. Others can find true contentment in finding work in an occupation. Still others may decide to dedicate time to pursue a hobby and further an interest. These are all perfect paths to express the soul's inner roots.

One should not only decide to follow their soul's inner roots but should also have faith in its true importance. Actualizing the soul brings one to true happiness and contentment as well as to fulfillment of the will of the Creator, who created them in a certain way for a certain reason. Thus, when a person follows their soul into action, they're fulfilling their destiny and playing the role in creation that they were made to play. By doing so, they're perfecting the creation and strengthening the will of God in the world, effecting great spiritual and positive change in their world and to their surroundings.

Expressing the soul doesn't only come in the form of careers or hobbies; it also manifests in individual actions and situations. The honest thoughts and feelings that come to a person who is connected to their soul's root and is used to having an inner dialogue with themselves as they go about their days, will reflect in their actions.

This concept is best illustrated with a few simple examples. Someone who feels a desire to be kind should allow themselves to be kind. This kindness can manifest in smiling at a cashier in a store or giving charity to a poor person on the street. But expression of the soul can come in many other forms. Someone who finds themselves wronged in a certain business transaction or social interaction should stand up for themselves, if that's what they feel inside. They should let themselves speak their truth, even if the truth is to tell someone else, "Hey, what you did isn't right!"

Express the Inner Truths of Your Soul

Shape Your Life According to Your Soul's Qualities

Following the soul should not normally be overly radical or against the ethics of our forefathers; rather they should be based on wholly good attributes such as kindness, truth, justice, understanding, and so on.

Simply put, you should let yourself be who you are and express the inner truths of your soul.

One should shape their lives according to their soul's qualities. Someone who has a passion for beautiful buildings may find their destiny by working as a contractor and designing and building beautiful houses or even skyscrapers. Someone who has a fascination with the law of the land and a passion for justice should study law and take the cases that will bring justice and positive outcomes to the world. Someone who finds relaxation behind the wheel of a vehicle may find happiness being a truck driver, spending endless hours on the roads.

The options and paths are endless. Some will make careers out of their inner findings that will leave them satisfied working day in and day out in a certain field, while others need only a few minutes every week to express a certain positive aspect of their soul and then dedicate the majority of their working time to another field. An example is a person who decides to learn to play a musical instrument, sing, dance, paint, or write poetry. Their main passion may be in a different area, but they allow themselves to express certain aspects of their soul by setting aside time to pursue other interests. These expressions are also very important, not only for the individual's happiness but for deeper hidden spiritual benefits that are brought to the world through them.

What is One's Main Path in Life?

Build It on Solid Self-Understanding, Know Yourself

A person's main path in life should be built on solid self-understanding. The more you know about yourself, the clearer your path is.

Someone learning these teachings for the first time may come to superficial conclusions. "I'll be a makeup artist! Or a chef!" they may think to themselves, while these conclusions are just a result of hasty thoughts and uncultivated desires and motivations.

The truth is, there are people who are truly meant to be makeup artists and chefs. They will be deeply happy to make up the faces of new brides and event goers every day, or to find absolute fulfillment cooking delicious and satisfying meals for others.

Some are born to learn and teach Torah. Their love and fascination with Jewish Law will allow them to spend endless hours in the study halls delving into the opinions of the sages of the past. They will form precise conclusions that they will be able to pass easily to their students, who will be inspired by their love of Torah to also love Torah themselves.

Some will be attracted to learning about the spiritual side of existence and finding the answers to their deepest questions in kabbalists' books of past generations, and be content with finding a simple job to work during the day to bring income to their families.

Others will yearn endlessly for a deeper and more revealed connection with their souls and the Creator, and find a good portion of time every day to spend in personal prayer, aiming their intentions and holy desires to the King of all Kings.

The best way is to find a path that correlates with who you are at the root of your soul and allows you to sustain yourself materially; to find a career or job that aligns with your natural character and interests, while also leaving aside space to pursue any other hobbies that you feel drawn towards.

Fulfill Your Destiny

Put Your Soul's Truths Into The World Of Action

A person fulfills their destiny by being who the Creator made them to be at the root of their soul. Wherever a person finds themselves in life, they should take the steps that they can to put their soul's truths into the world of action.

The more people who follow the path outlined in this chapter, the more empowered others will be to do the same. In time, the world will return to being as it was created to be, a true expression of the Creator's will. The final culmination of the world will be a complete return to the Creator's will, where every human being will be expressing their true nature and living a life that is an expression of their soul's root.

This final culmination will enable Redemption Day to take place. A description of Redemption Day will follow in the next chapter.

HOW TO FIND YOURSELF
THE PRACTICAL PATH

Prayer: Personal Prayer & Written Prayer

There is one tool that is central to taking this advice into practice. That tool is personal prayer. In this section, we'll explain what it is, how to do it, provide examples, and describe the fantastic rewards of what is undoubtedly the greatest single spiritual practice.

The practice of personal prayer is relatively newly revived but is very ancient. Ancient teachings describe the great forefathers Avraham, Isaac, and Jacob as being responsible for instituting the three daily prayers. Today, Jews recognize these as the written prayers that were canonized by the sages of the Second Temple — the *Amida*. But let's think realistically, could they have been saying the *Amida* prayer thousands of years before the sages wrote them? Of course not.

The prayers our forefathers prayed were personal. They spoke to God spontaneously from the heart, expressing their feelings, hopes, and greatest holy desires. This tradition of personal prayer continued through the generations up until the exile of the Jewish Nation in the days of Ezra. Rambam, Rabbi Moshe ben Maimon, describes this in detail in *Mishnah Torah, Laws of Prayer, Law 1*.

During the exile of the Jewish people, this holy practice of personal prayer was widely lost and forgotten. Because of the radical spiritual decline of Israel that happened in exile, the sages of the Second Temple codified a written prayer. As described by Rambam in the section quoted above, the sages did this for two reasons. Firstly, Israel was living among foreign nations. The knowledge of the Hebrew language was declining sharply, and a standard prayer in Hebrew was adopted to preserve the knowledge of the language. Secondly, the sages instituted the written prayer to preserve the memory of the concept of prayer forever. So no matter where they went throughout the long exile, they would always know about the concept of prayer and could practice it to a certain degree. They sought to preserve the knowledge that the Creator could be reached through the supplication of speech.

They saw that true knowledge of prayer and the holy language of Hebrew was vanishing before their eyes, so they decreed this standardized formal prayer be adopted by all Jews. This written prayer, the *Amida*, has been preserved by Jews across the world until today.

But the personal prayer practiced by our forefathers and described by Rambam was virtually lost during the long exile. Israel did pray, but it was through the words of the prayer book.

Hitbodedut: Self-Seclusion

A little over two hundred years ago, personal prayer was reintroduced to the public of Israel after almost two thousand years. Rebbe Nachman of Breslov taught his students the true meaning of prayer, the ancient practice of our ancestors. He called it *Hitbodidut*, which means "self-seclusion" in Hebrew.

He taught that *Hitbodidut* is the highest path of them all and the most effective path to truly connect with the Creator and the hidden spiritual aspects of one's soul. "Take it!" he told his followers, adding that it's very important to spend a full hour dedicated to this practice daily.

His lessons contain much explanation about how to do this. Above all, he makes it very clear that this practice of personal prayer is the main tool (along with Torah study) in forging a conscious, individual connection with the Creator and in affecting real change in the world as a result of petitions being answered.

Because Rebbe Nachman revealed personal prayer to his students after he discovered it, and because of the great efforts he took to explain how to properly do it and the effects and importance of it, it has been able to find its way into the pages of this book. Personal prayer is truly the main way to bring the advice in this chapter into effective action in the proper direction (the way that is the truth).

How to Pray

The first step of personal prayer is to have faith that the Creator can hear you and that your prayers are effective. If you don't believe that you're getting through to the Creator, you can't truly pray. Some people may honestly not have this faith; there is a solution for this that will be discussed later. The reality is, however, that the Creator hears every word.

Think about it logically. How could an infinite, omnipresent being not hear you?

The next step is to have the confidence that He listens, that He cares. The short answer is that He cares more than you can imagine. The Creator's infinite love extends to all of His Creations, as He carved their souls from His essence. We are His children. He cares for and loves all, even more so those who choose the highest purpose of Creation — to seek Him amidst the barriers of physicality that block His presence from us. Even those who feel the burden of their sins and the years they spent in the darkness, walking in bent and twisted paths far from thoughts of spirituality. The Creator's love and desire are especially for these people who choose to seek Him despite their past mistakes. He loves such people greatly.

Once a person has faith that the Creator is listening to their prayers, loves them, and treasures their prayers, they can pray effectively with proper confidence.

Let's now discuss a few important aspects of effective personal prayer.

Spoken Speech

The first thing to note is that personal prayer must be done out loud. It's not enough to just think of your prayers. That would be considered thinking, not praying. True prayer is only done through audible speech. When praying to the Creator, you must talk to Him.

There are very deep Kabbalistic understandings of why prayer must be done through human speech as opposed to just thought, but those explanations are beyond the focus of this book. With that said, a simple hint as to why speech is so important can be found in Genesis. We see that the Creator spoke the world into being, He didn't think it into being. There is a profound mystery to speech and its importance and effectiveness in personal prayer.

Speaking might be uncomfortable for the beginner. They might say to themselves, "God can also hear my thoughts! I don't have to speak out loud, that's silly." While of course the Creator can hear our thoughts, it would be best for this person to understand with humility that there is much that is beyond their understanding, and even though they don't grasp the reason why speech is so important, they should go to a private and quiet place and begin speaking. They will come to a higher level of honesty, humility, and true faith by doing this.

Honesty

Truthful prayers are the only ones that reach the Creator. "Truthful" means that they are an honest expression of one's true desires. In other words, they are not praying prayers that they think the Creator wants to hear, or acting, or pretending to themselves or Him in any way with their words, tone, or attitude. They are simply being real and honest. The greatest detector of truth is oneself; every person knows exactly when they're being real, and when they're pretending. Strive to be as real and honest as you can. You will know when you are.

Perhaps someone knows that it's good to pray for something, but doesn't honestly want it. For example, they often catch themselves gossiping about others, and they know it's very wrong to do so. But honestly (and unfortunately) it gives them a lot of enjoyment to speak about others behind their backs. If such a person were to pray, "God, I don't want to gossip anymore! Please help me to stop," this wouldn't be a full, honest expression of the truth. An honest prayer would be, "God, I have a serious issue. I gossip. I know it's wrong and I should stop, but I like to do it. Please help me." In this second prayer, the person is admitting the real situation and asking God to help. That makes it a true prayer.

Being truthful with God and oneself is a great key to prayer. One must be expressing one's soul as honestly as possible. Admitting the truth is vital. In terms of our example above, the prayer "God, help me to *want* to stop gossiping" is a thousand times better than "God, I want to stop gossiping" when the latter is not the truth.

The Creator pays attention to such details. One who is exacting in their honesty during prayer is walking the true path.

Focus and Desire

Focus and desire are essential to effective prayer. The focus of the mind can be a difficult thing. Thoughts easily wander and attention is lost. While praying, one must make a conscious effort to focus and refocus their mind on the words they're saying and the train of thought that is leading their words.

Desire is also vital. Desire and passion of the heart must be awakened during prayer. Simply put, one should want what they are praying for. Wanting is desire itself, and this the tool of the heart.

Without wanting what one is praying for, they're not prayers at all — more like empty words.

The desire of the heart is what powers the prayers to reach God in a spiritual way.

For example, if a child asks his father for something, but the father knows the child doesn't actually want it, why would he give it to him? Why would the father give it to him if he doesn't care about it? But, if the child comes before his father and asks for something he wants, the father sees the passion in his eyes and is happy to give him what he wants because he knows it will make him happy. The child will be grateful for the gift and will grow to love his father in a greater way because he witnessed his kindness. The father also receives great satisfaction from being able to give his child what he wants. This example provides a clear illustration of why desire is so necessary for prayer.

What about a person who fails to find the passion and desire they feel is necessary for prayer? In this very lacking they can find themselves a great source of passion and desire: namely, that they want to have more passion and desire in their prayers. In this way, their perceived lacking itself becomes a source of pure prayer.

Waking up true desire on other issues can be a challenge, but it simply requires effort and self-examination. Surely someone who feels apathetic on the issue they want to pray about actually does care about the issue, or else they wouldn't want to pray about it in the first place. Many times, a lack of desire is just an obstacle, and once the person dives deeper and faces their true motives they find they honestly do care about the issue they came to pray about and can pray freely and honestly about it with a lot of passion and strength.

Personal prayer can be viewed as an exercise of the soul. Using the tools of the mind and heart, a person can push their mind to focus and their heart to yearn and desire for the things they ask for. This concept of spiritual effort is very important. It is the process that detaches the materialism that blocks the mind and heart from connecting to the Creator in a hidden spiritual way.

Time and Perseverance

Personal prayer should be a daily practice, up to one hour in duration. Someone who starts at ten or fifteen minutes should work their way to a longer time. The more time one has, the more they can investigate their motives, desires, prayers, and issues on a deeper level. Someone who only dedicates five to ten minutes every day to personal prayer rushes through their list of desires and only superficially covers the things they wanted to talk about.

A longer session allows for more in depth focus on the issues at hand and effective covering of much more ground. Remember, the Creator pays attention to detail and specificity. Someone who is not rushed can delve into the topics of prayer they wanted to speak about. They can come to conclusions that shed light on their issues. They can turn these findings into deeper and more effective prayers that awaken their heart's desire in a greater and more honest way. This makes more effective prayers which "move the heart" of the Creator to answer them and impart even greater light and understanding. Examples of this will be provided below.

One should make their prayer a daily practice and have complete faith that their prayers are being heard by the Creator. They should not let themselves be discouraged by any negative thoughts that their prayers are not working. Even if they don't feel themselves making progress or find themselves being answered, they should not desist in the slightest. Rather, they should continue with complete faith, returning to the principles of prayer outlined in this chapter.

Those who continue will no doubt see results, and those who have longer prayers will see greater results. Especially for those who dedicate longer time to prayer, every moment doesn't have to be filled with words. Honest, focused words are greater than uninspired rambling. Ideally, this time should be for meditative prayer, in which one delves into their soul to find their honest and pure desires and brings them out in speech.

Place and Privacy

Personal prayer should ideally be done in a quiet, private place, especially by beginners. It needs to be done in a place where a person can focus, free of distraction and away from others. Rebbe Nachman suggested his followers walk in the forests at night, away from paths that people regularly walk.

This way, they won't lose their focus or concentration if someone else crosses their path.

Nature is a fantastic and inspiring place to pray, but a person can also find an effective location in a private room in their house. The main thing is that it is private and free of distraction, so they can more easily focus and feel comfortable to be themselves and express themselves completely honestly before God.

In conclusion, faith that God is listening, honesty, focus, desire, perseverance, liberal time, location, and privacy are very important aspects of prayer. Much more about personal prayer can be found in the writings of Rebbe Nachman and his students. In the next few chapters, we will explain additional aspects of prayer and provide examples about how it can be used to arrive at one's soul's root and create a path of expression in the world (as discussed in the sections on Steps One and Two of the repentance process). Personal prayer also has other beneficial aspects which will be touched on and briefly explained with examples.

To understand how personal prayer can be used to return to one's soul's root, an additional explanation of it by Rebbe Nachman is very useful. Numerous times in his teachings, Rebbe Nachman calls personal prayer *Yishuv HaDaat*. Translated, it means "setting one's mind/being." Elsewhere he describes it as having a conversation with oneself.

Having a conversation with oneself brings a whole new aspect to the concept of personal prayer. Instead of just "shooting arrows to Heaven" in the form of prayers and requests to

Heaven, one can have an intimate conversation with themselves. This is vital to connecting to the true root of your soul.

Someone who is trying to connect with their true qualities might use this time of personal prayer to probe themselves deeply about their past to find hints that shed light on their search. "What are my true interests?" they might ask themselves. The next thought that comes into their mind could be a memory from high school or college of a class they truly enjoyed. "I remember that class!" they will tell themselves, and then ask, "Is that my true interest?"

The key is to always go deeper. "Why did I like that class? At its core, what was the thing that sparked my imagination or piqued my interest?" The answers will come in the form of spontaneous and natural thoughts.

In the way described above, a person can have a conversation with themselves that flows through different topics, leading them to deeper realizations and accurate conclusions. The key is to ask, question, search, and listen to the answers that come from within. These are the answers that come from the soul. By having deep conversations with yourself, you can discover the true roots of your soul and clearly understand what exactly makes you happy, sad, free, imprisoned, inspired, motivated, and more. In this way, prayer can be a powerful tool for solving personal problems.

In fact, personal prayer is probably the most powerful tool for solving personal problems and issues. Through conversing with God and oneself, a person can locate the root of their issue, come up with a plan or methods to solve it, and ask for assistance from the Almighty, in one fluid conversation.

Following is a few examples:

Take a scenario where a man is having serious problems finding a wife. He goes on many dates, but every time, one thing or another ruins his chances with the girl. He goes on a walk around his neighborhood late one night, when no one else is normally on the streets.

"God. Please help me!" he begins. "I never make progress on my dates. After a few dates, the women are no longer interested. I don't know where I go wrong. I always get so nervous that it might get serious or else go sideways." Then he realizes, "I get nervous... And when I get nervous my whole personality changes, and it's very hard for me to express myself naturally. I shut down emotionally." He reflects.

"Maybe I need to face my fears and force myself to get out of my nervous bubble. That feels like a real answer," he concludes. "Also, I need to remember that everything happens for a reason. The fact that I haven't been married yet means I haven't met my true soul mate. I need to have faith through this process."

"God!" he calls out as he walks. "Please. I'm asking you. Bring me to my true soul mate in the easiest way. Help me to remain calm as I find the right one. Help me to have the courage and ability to express my true self despite any anxiety I have. Also, help me to not be so anxious in the first place!" he prays.

See how this man is naturally expressing himself in personal prayer? He comes to the prayer with a problem, narrows down the roots of his issues, comes to solid conclusions about how to address the situation, and finally, expresses it all in an honest prayer from the heart.

These types of prayers —that shed light on a situation and ask for help in executing a realistic plan of action — are prayers that God listens to. They are strong prayers that have a greater likelihood of being answered.

In another scenario, a man struggling to control his anger goes to walk in a private part of a public park in his neighborhood. He begins having a conversation with himself.

"I don't know what to do! I did it again. I freaked out on my children again. I get so angry..." He sighs. "I don't know why I'm not controlling myself. Can I even control myself?" He thinks deeply for a few moments until a truthful thought comes to him. "Yes. I think I can control myself. Sometimes I feel so much pressure I let myself lose control. But even in those moments, I am letting myself lose control, so that means deep down I am in control," he concludes. "But I get so stressed..."

He considers for a minute. "Why do I get so stressed from certain situations? I'm so involved in the moment that it's hard to take a step back and breathe. But honestly, why can't I just do that? Take a step back in those situations and relax for a moment? I think I can really, I just forget to." The realization hits him. "That's what I need to do. I need to just step back, relax, breathe, and not focus so much on my stress and pressure in the heat of the moment. I just need to take time to withdraw myself from the situation when I feel the pressure," he determines.

"God," he prays, "I am truly sorry I let anger get the best of me. Please forgive me and please let my loved ones forgive me as well."

Through this conversation, the person is able to reach important conclusions about himself and a path to help him not make the same mistakes.

Such conversations are so vital and effective in personal problem solving. The wisdom they yield is perfectly tailored for the individual because it's coming from within their soul itself.

Prayer to God

The Way To Return to One's Roots

Self Improvement goes hand in hand with connecting to the root of one's soul. To explain it esoterically, the Divine soul of a person is always connected to them, but because of the materialistic nature of this world, their inherent connection is blocked from their perception. They are connected to their soul on the deepest and highest levels, but they can't feel or sense it. Yet as they work to remove their imperfect character traits, their connection to the root of their soul is revealed. Gradually, their true character begins to shine. Their inherent goodness can express itself honestly as they reject the bad traits that disconnected them from their true being.

Simply put, when a person realizes deep down that they have been insecure for a long time, that they have been wearing a false mask in their interpersonal interactions to hide their insecurities, they are then able to feel themselves be more authentic.

Take someone who deeply loves to paint. Painting brings them true joy and inner satisfaction, but as a teen they were told by their parents that painting is a waste of time and won't help them be successful in the long run. When they go back to their true selves they will begin to paint once again.

Take someone who fights a temptation to look at immodest sights on the streets or the internet. They will detach themselves from these base desires that block the holy and pure light of their soul from shining through their body into everyday life.

Take someone who struggles with apathy for the world around them. Forcing themselves to pay attention to the needs of others will awaken the inner kindness that surely lies within.

By these examples, we can infer many more, and we see that self-improvement is directly connected to this greater goal of returning to one's true self.

Prayer to God and conversation with oneself is the way to return to one's roots. Before time is spent in prayer and self evaluation, all inner connections to one's soul are only hypothetical; personal prayer is the only way to find one's root, which is one's personal, palpable connection with God.

CHAPTER FIVE

The Final Redemption

Intro - The Timeline of Redemption

- The Redemption will be complete and total; it will take place in the lives of every living creature, including all plants and animals.

- Redemption will happen in the present moment and will sweep through the timeline of history.

- The Holy Temple will be rebuilt in Jerusalem and will be a house of prayer for all nations.

- The Lost Tribes of Israel will return to their true place.

- A world pilgrimage will take place where all people walk together to see the face of the Creator and call Him by His name at the site of the rebuilt Temple.

- All people will be sure of His position as the infinite source of all reality; the doubt and disagreements between faiths that plagued the world before will be no more.

- We will understand the story of the journey of our souls from Adam to us.

- Humanity will live for 1000 years of peace.

A Spiritual Shift to a Higher Dimension

Our Minds Over our Bodies - Individual To Omnipresent

All creatures, humans, and animals will enjoy the raising of the worlds. On that day, our minds will climb to a higher dimension to enjoy a perspective more revealing than we can obtain from within our bodies. The whole picture of life on earth will be open to seeing and perceiving.

Our perspective will shift from individual to omnipresent. That is, instead of each of us having a limited bodily perspective that only includes ourselves, our perspective will shift to one similar to the Creator's. The whole width and breath of Creation and all of the Creations existing in it will be experienced by every soul.

Timeline to Infinity

Everyone will understand their personal life situation is not a mere snapshot in time. Meaning, we will see our entire lives as continuing in all moments into infinity. It will be understood that our entire lives as well as the lives of previous generations are in continual existence from the perspective of the Creator.

From our perspective, every moment that is lived on earth is within a timeline—a timeline that begins at birth and ends at death. We go through life living in the present, experiencing life situations and events from moment to moment. From the Creator's infinite perspective above the timeline, every moment experienced on earth lasts forever. To Him, these moments in time are not in any past, present, or future, but they exist constantly.

When we rise to a dimension higher, we will experience the Creator's perspective. We will all be able to experience the timeline of all generations simultaneously as one. The lives of the millions and billions of people who lived before us will be open to us. In a moment, their entire lives will come before our perspective.

Not only in the realm of human beings will the Redemption come. The souls of all animals and creatures will rise on this holy day. Our souls will also perceive and experience, in a moment, the lives of the animals and creatures on earth. Every pair of eyes from the fish in the sea to the birds of the sky will be open to this holy spectacle.

When humanity rises from our personal perspectives to that higher dimension and becomes unified with the Creator, we will experience the world in complete perfection from behind the curtains. There will be no limitations of physicality.

The Greater Plan Understood Spiritually

The secret purpose behind the mundane and major occurrences in our lives will be understood by their purpose in the greater plan. The reason we once lost all our savings, the reason we moved houses, and all other experiences will be understood in the context of the Divine Plan. They will be understood in its spiritual aspects.

Which spiritual rectifications were accomplished by certain events and life situations will be comprehensible to us? Why we had chance encounters with seemingly complete strangers will be understood. For example, in a previous lifetime, certain souls may have had a disagreement; and by meeting in a supermarket and holding the door for each other, their previous disturbance was fixed. Entire books can be written on the understandings we will see clearly on the Day of Redemption.

All the life stories of all the generations since the days of Adam and Eve will be accounted for. The spiritual journeys of all the sparks of souls will be told, all the way back to Adam and Eve, the original souls from which we all come. Our grandparents' and great-grandparents' life stories will be revealed to our clear minds both physically and spiritually.

The spiritual root of our generations and the roles they played while on earth will be understood clearly. This shift of consciousness will allow all souls to experience the lives of other Creations. Our expanded consciousness will see through their very eyes.

Momentarily, we will become unified with the Creator, and this experience will be our perspective. We will realize and know who we really are in the root of our soul—meaning, the high and Divine aspect that our soul represents. All this will be revealed in our lifetime. The spiritual secrets that are behind everything in existence will be understood.

The spiritual causes of all reincarnations, physical actions, and even chance meetings will be open and understood. The physicality that has blocked us from seeing the spiritual reality for so long will finally be uncovered. The world we inhabit will be freed from all the coverings that block our knowledge and understanding of its true nature and purpose. Everything that has ever happened in this world has a spiritual cause that will be revealed on this holy day.

This vast experience of earth's existence will be open and perceived all at once during the rising of the souls. We will see through all of the worlds that ever existed. We will see their lives and understand all of their purposes.

Our minds will reach deep and complete understandings of who we are and what role we had in the giant and complex system of the Creation. This will lead us to become united with all other souls, and together we will see the Silver Eternal Sea of Souls. We will look down from our high perspectives and see a silver mirror reflecting the higher worlds, and we will realize we are a reflection of those higher worlds.

In the Perspective of the Creator, There Is no Time

As discussed earlier, every individual lives their life centered in their personal "time-tunnel." They go through life operating from their limited perspective, living from moment to moment. Days and years go by for the entirety of their lives. This individual makes up one "world." During the life of this individual, there are billions of other "worlds" who are living in their own time tunnels. Combine this with the trillions of animals, insects, fish, and all other creatures that also exist at the same time. Now, take into account the thousands of years for which life has existed on earth and the time tunnels of all who have ever lived.

In the perspective of the Creator, there is no time. All of life as we know it on earth is being experienced in the constant present moment of the Creator. Every shout of joy, every apology since the beginning of time is being lived in the present moment from His perspective. All of the past since the Creation of Adam and Eve is being eternally played out in the higher perspective which is above time.

This redemption will not only occur in the present moment when we experience this shift, the redemption will redeem every moment in history, perfecting the past in every way possible.

The Completion of All the Worlds:

The Redemption Will Sweep the Timeline of Human History

The redemption will be the correction and completion of all the worlds. Every moment in time throughout history can be called an individual world. The explanation follows, in every moment the world as a whole is in a current state of being. Sometimes there are large wars, sometimes there are celebrations. In every moment, the world is at a collective state composed of almost endless smaller events and perspectives, and each of these moments is called a world.

All the worlds combined, every moment together, is called "all the worlds". All the worlds are the complete picture of every perspective of every moment in time. It is like the complete representation of the Creator's light that has been shining on us from the earliest days of Creation, the ultimate "big picture".

Like we said above, the final redemption will be a correction and completion of "All the worlds". This means that every collective moment, composed of every individual perspective, even to the scale of every cell and particle, will be redeemed in totality. From the earliest days of Creation up to and including the moments leading up to redemption, all moments and all of the parts of each giant collective moment will be redeemed and corrected.

Every fraction of time will be redeemed, and we will experience the redemption in its totality, and not just from our perspectives. This complete correction of all the worlds will also give evil what it deserves once and for all. All the evil that has happened since the beginning of the world has never been forgotten. Just as every pure and innocent thing throughout history will be rewarded on redemption day, so too will every evil choice be eternally punished.

The Reward of Every Moment Depends on Our Actions

Every Individual's Reward

Like we discussed, redemption will sweep the entire timeline of human history, in every moment and situation. But not every moment of every person will be redeemed. The redemption of every individual's moment depends on how (or if) they were worthy of being in the general redemption at that specific time.

The explanation follows, the redemption will be the completion and perfection of every situation in every moment of time. So every person's moments will be redeemed based on their place in every moment. When the redemption sweeps the timeline of human history, if they were on the "good side" of Creation during that moment during that time, they will be redeemed. If they were not, or in the darkness of evil, they will not be redeemed and they will be corrected if the truth of the situation calls for it.

For example, if someone was hurting someone else, they will be embarrassed in the moment, while the abused will find their redemption and see justice being served in that moment.

The people whose actions are deemed worthy of being redeemed, and they will experience the perfection of that moment and all the spiritual bounty and reward of being righteous in that moment.

So most people will have many moments of their lives that will be redeemed, and others will not. For example, when the redemption comes, someone who had only two moments of their life that were worthy to be redeemed will experience spiritual elevation and bounty in those two moments. They will live eternally in those two moments, experiencing the great spiritual reward of the good they did.

It's important to understand that every moment is a world onto itself of eternal bounty and spiritual satisfaction. So even someone who only did two good things in their life will have great and eternal reward and enjoyment from their actions.

There Will be Some Who Will Not be Redeemed at All

There will be some who will not be redeemed at all, in any moment of their life. These are the most evil people, whose entire existence was evil and hated by those around them. Even if they were nice or friendly to people at some times in their life, it was only for selfish and manipulative reasons. These evil people whose only justice will be served by being erased from the world completely and from all those around them, will descend into the depths of hell during redemption. Their eternal suffering will serve as their debt to humanity, and their hell will be the fire of the core that supplies warmth to the rest of humanity for thousands of years of redemption.

The actions that make someone worthy of redemption are when they were on the "good side" of the Creator. Times when they were doing good things create moments of redemption. For example, even a simple act of throwing a piece of trash into its proper receptacle rather than littering can tip the scale of merit to one's favor. Thinking about the Creator and thinking how one can perform actions of Divine Service create everlasting moments of connection with the Creator.

The depth of the merit in every moment will result in a fuller bounty of reward, and it depends on the depth of the person's intention, or greatness of their action. For example, someone who does something small to benefit another person, like holding a door for them, may experience an everlasting reward for that small action. But if there was a great and sincere intention of benevolence attached to the action, the reward will be greater.

Learning Torah, Levels of Spirituality

Moments spent fulfilling the Creator's commandments will certainly be moments of redemption and great spiritual satisfaction. One who fulfills his obligation absentmindedly will still be rewarded for his service, but one who fulfills the same obligation with great devotion and love of God will certainly gain more merit, and thereby greater reward, once the moment is redeemed.

Only the worthy moments of a person's life will enjoy the eternal elevation of redemption. The moments that are not worthy, won't be redeemed, and as mentioned above, the moments of true evil will be punished eternally.

The worthiness of a moment to be redeemed is based on what the person was doing in that moment. If, in the moment, they were connecting to the Creator in their thoughts or actions, performing *Mitzvot*, or doing good deeds, that moment is worthy of redemption. In the time of redemption, these moments will be an open access to spiritual growth and bounty for the person.

Time Will "Expand"

The question arises: How will we be able to experience all of these redeemed moments at once? When the Redemption comes, the entire Creation will be shifted to a higher level that transcends the dimensions of time and physical space.

In our current perspective, as described above, we are limited to experiencing life in the present moment. Even though we are souls carved from infinity, we are limited to experience life in the present moment. Even though the past is in our memory, we can't actually relive it currently. We are limited to experiencing it only through our imagination which is the memory of what happened. The future is also beyond inaccessible to us. We can only predict or try to plan how it will unfold. It is also limited to be perceived through our imagination. In our current days, all that we truly have is the present moment.

But when the final redemption comes and the timeline of human history is redeemed according to truth and justice, our souls will ascend beyond the limitations of time, and we will be able to experience all the moments that have been redeemed. Currently we cannot think or experience two moments at once, but when the redemption happens, there will be no obstacles for us to be able to perceive all of these moments. But we will not only be able to experience the moments of our own lives that will be redeemed, we will also be able to "travel" and experience others moments of Creation that we have a connection to.

Circles of Connection

Our access to experience the redemption and all its moments will not only be limited to the moments of our own life that were worthy to be redeemed. We will also have access to the moments of others and other parts of Creation that we have some sort of connection with.

For example, if we gave some sort of good life advice to a person who went on to use that advice successfully for their own benefit or the benefit of others, we will have a connection to their success and their moments of redemption that are connected with our effect on their life.

In another aspect, we are intimately connected with our ancestors, and all of their moments of redemption will be accessible and shared by us, and likewise they have shares in all of our success. Likewise, we will be able to "travel back" and experience the moments of our greatest ancestors who are the heroes of the Bible and ultimately in our father Jacob, the forefather to the nation of Israel, and to our forefathers Isaac and Avraham, all the way back to Adam and Eve.

The circles of connection that will open our supernal minds to many experiences of redemption outside our personal ones are very broad and wide. They expand based on our connection with others, interests in the physical world, and much more.

A main thing to realize is very few will be left "empty handed" on redemption day with "small portions". A vast majority of people will have generous and wide, miraculously expanded circles of connection that will allow them access and experience of huge portions of redemption that spans across time and place.

Resurrection of the Dead

The redemption of the entire timeline of human history, where all good moments will be redeemed is the main concept of the Resurrection of the Dead. This is because when redemption comes, all that was in the "past" will be resurrected and live once again as we described. Death will cease to exist and all the redeemed moments of people's lives will be relieved constantly in spiritual bliss and perfection.

While the personal redemption of some people might involve their loved ones literally standing up from their graves, the main fulfillment of this prophecy will be to have the lives of all the dead resurrected from the past in eternal redemption.

Following the redemption of the worlds, life that follows it will be perfect and miraculous. The happiness, joy, and satisfaction in the streets will be a global festival. Every person with a musical instrument will play with joy, every person who can move to the rhythm will let it surge through their bodies. This is the destination of Creation: to rejoice in completion. All false beliefs and institutions will collapse and the truth will prevail as a result of the revelation of the Creator's supremacy. Idols will be thrown away—money, vanity, pride, everything that distracts us from our true purpose.

You Don't Need to be Jewish to Enjoy the Redemption

Every being will be included in this ultimate joy. The Jews might serve in the Temple, they might welcome everyone into the service; but everyone will be included in the ultimate redemption. Also, the Ten Lost Tribes of Israel will awaken from between the nations of the world and return to their homeland.

In the same way our lives today are permeated with normal occurrences, in the time of the Final Redemption, our lives will be filled with miracles that negate the natural functions of the universe. We will witness wonders. Each individual will realize their dreams alongside their loved ones. Truth will be revealed in all its glory, revealing to all of reality that the Creator is sovereign over everything. If a person wishes to fly, he will touch the sky. Miracles will be commonplace in the same way that running errands like grocery shopping, paying bills, or going to work is common today. But each miracle, instead of helping you overcome a negative situation, will help you realize your true purpose and manifest your innermost desires. You will see your precious dreams fulfilled before your eyes. In every detail, you will recognize a manifestation of Divine grace, proof of the Creator's control, and unconditional love. Each person will benefit from the perfection of the Creator's supervision over every detail of their life. You and your loved ones, whoever wishes to be near you, will be happy with you.

The Merit of Those People who Rise to Trust in the Creator

All the people of the world will see and understand the change in the Creator's supervision of His creation and turn their hearts toward goodness and unity. Brotherhood will be the lot of all the creatures of the world. All the people of the world will wish to receive the face of the Creator in the Land of Israel and the Holy City of Jerusalem, in the house of the great and wonderful name that will be called the Temple of

Prayer. It will be discovered by the masses. And all the creatures of the world will come to see the wonders of the Creator. Each one of them will see their Creator Himself. The pilgrimage will be undertaken not only by humans but also by animals. Herds of animals from across the world will travel together to Jerusalem. They will cross the expanses of terrain to pay homage to the Creator in the place He chooses.

These days will be revealed to us because we hold on to our belief that the Creator is observing our lives today. On the merit of those people who rise to trust in the Creator, to fulfill the task we were given, to reveal each one of His blessed qualities, virtues, and abilities that He bestowed upon us. Because of them, we will see wonders, Providence will be experienced in all aspects of life. We'll see miracles, money in our pockets… whatever we need will find us. We will look in the mirror and see the light of true joy shining.

No More Sorrow, No More Pain

It Will be Built Through our Faith and Prayer

The redemption will mean the global recognition of His unity and sovereignty. There will be no shortcomings, no war, no competition. Anyone who has a good and pure heart will enjoy the grace of the Creator. And who are those whose hearts are pure? It's you and me. We all have a pure heart. We, humans, want to be good for everyone. We do not want competition. We have a place in our hearts for everyone, when everyone behaves in a proper manner and as an ideal human. With our faith, we are protecting the world. Through us, the Creator will be revealed—thanks to the facts that we have not succumbed to the illusion of Nature and the events of the world, and that we never let the world mislead our hearts, and that each of us calls upon the Creator. Those who need healing will be healed, both in mind and body. Those who err will understand their mistakes.

On the morning of Redemption, you will find at your feet the most beautiful and comfortable shoes you have ever worn, along with an immaculate outfit of clothes to wear. You will live in a house where you want to live, surrounded by neighbors among whom you want to live. Birds will chirp and greet you in flight. Squirrels, hedgehogs, deer, all kinds of creatures greeting you as their friend. Everything will brighten. So, it will be in all countries across the world, countless people all knowing the Creator, saying, "The Lord is God." On the beach, seals will clap fins and dolphins will accompany those who want to swim further. All the colors of the rainbow and the beauty of creation will be visible to all, and this will be Providence. All creatures, regardless of their species, will live in harmonious cooperation. Rich, succulent fruit will be served to all open mouths. Flowers, sunshine, and butterflies will appear before your eyes wherever you gaze.

And so shall we live forever, as death will no longer be a factor. There will be no more sorrow, no more pain. This will be the redemption. And it is realized and built every second, through our faith and prayer.

CHAPTER SIX

Redemption &
The Secret of Repentance

Redemption and The Secret of Repentance

The beautiful vision of Redemption described in the previous chapter is a holy vision of the future. For thousands of years, we have been waiting for this holy day to come. In this chapter, we will explain how the Day of Redemption is connected with the secret of repentance.

The verse states וקראתם דרור בארץ "Proclaim freedom throughout the land" for the *Yovel* (Jubilee) year. This is the year when Hebrew slaves are freed from their masters and land is returned to the family who originally inherited it. It is a time when debts are forgiven and all is returned to its original place in Creation.

In the *Yovel* year, slaves return to their rightful place, which is to be free. The Day of Redemption is compared to the *Yovel* year in that the same concept of freedom will apply similarly. On the Day of Redemption, the entire world including all humanity will come back to its rightful place, which is to be free to be their true selves and fill their rightful role in the world.

Another verse says לקרא להם דרור "Proclaim liberty among them" in reference to freeing Hebrew slaves. In our current generation, much of the world can be considered slaves in certain ways. The root of many people's slavery is fear. They are slaves to their fears, and this manifests in many aspects of their lives. Most people, for example, are scared of others' opinions or judgment. They allow themselves to be enslaved by the norms of society and choose to follow the crowd rather than live their lives differently. They're scared to be different, and so they live by the boundaries of their fears instead of following the truth of their soul, which beckons them to a different path.

On Redemption Day, the entire world will be freed from the slavery of their fears and will be happily empowered to live according to the truth of their souls.

Instead Of Being Free To Be Who They Want To Be; They Let The World Enslave Them

We find in the Torah that there is a negative connotation associated with the slave, especially the slave who chooses to continue to be a slave even after their freedom is possible. There is a ritual the Torah prescribes to such a slave: Their ear is pierced by their master. The *Gemara* (Kiddushin 22b) asks why specifically the ear is prescribed to be pierced and not another part of the body. Rabban Yochanan ben Zakai answers that it was the ears that heard the Creator's voice on Mt. Sinai saying, "For to Me the children of Israel are slaves" (Vayikra 25:55). Since this person chooses to continue to serve an earthly master (a human being) instead of grasping their freedom to serve their true, Divine Master, their ear should be pierced. This shows disrespect for their decision to remain a slave.

The true will of the Creator, like the verse above, is that we will be free of any earthly masters and serve Him alone. To choose to remain a servant of earthly masters, in whatever form they are, is not a decision that is respected by the Creator. This is why the slave's ear is pierced when they return to their master.

When people choose to be a slave of this world, they let their fears guide their lives. They "sell" themselves to the society around them, to the opinions of others, and they are considered to be enslaved by the world. They are not free to choose what they want to do or how they want to live their lives. Instead, they let their fears guide their decisions and path in life.

These people wear clothes which they think will be liked by those around them. They choose professions for similar reasons. They act and behave in a way that they think will be liked or respected. They blend in and follow whatever social norms are prevalent at the time, and don't contradict them, even if they feel inside that something is wrong. They do all this simply because they're scared of doing the opposite. Instead of being free to be who they want to be, they let the world enslave them.

The Opposite of What Our Creator Wants for Us

This way of living life is wrong. It's not the way we're meant to live; it's the opposite of what the Creator wants for us and of what we should want for ourselves.

When the Final Redemption comes, "freedom will be proclaimed throughout the land." All those who were slaves to their fears will be set free. The shackles of fear that gripped so many souls and enslaved them to this world will be broken, and everyone will finally be able to find their true role in Creation according to the spiritual root of their soul, in the process discussed in Chapters 4 and 5.

In our generation, before this massive revelation of humanity will take place, most people are not fulfilling their born-to-be role in Creation. Because they've been enslaved by this world, they let fear be the main guide of their lives instead of following their inner truth with faith. Their masters are society, their communities, families, associates, friends, and so on.

Because they let fear lead their lives, they are constantly going against the true design of the Creator. For example, people choose careers based on their parents' wishes instead of their interests and passions. They're scared to disappoint their parents or go against their wishes. They find themselves working in a field of work that was never meant for them because they didn't follow the truth of their soul. Other people get married before they want to, or choose to learn full-time in a Torah academy, even though inside their souls are screaming in defiance of these decisions. Despite their souls' truths leading them in different directions, they choose to follow these paths that are not meant for them.

Before "freedom is proclaimed," many of our actions and decisions are based on fear, pressure, and anxiety, instead of being true expressions of our soul like those discussed in Chapter 5.

But when "freedom is proclaimed," the invitation is open to us to come back to our true selves, to live lives based on our true paths, and to return to our rightful roles in Creation. For example, those who have a passion for the anatomy of the human body will feel empowered to learn to become doctors, despite their parents' wishes that they become great Torah scholars. Those who are meant to be graphic designers will follow their passion and add beauty and positive change to the world with their designs. True chefs will cook, and their meals will rejuvenate the bodies and souls of all who eat their food. Born-to-be pilots will finally be able to fly the planes they were born to fly. Every corner of Creation will be perfect and fit its true place.

By the spiritual power of this movement, whereby the entire world will come to their true selves, the Final Redemption will come.

Messiah

This movement will only occur through the true Messiah. The Zohar says that Moses is the Messiah. Why does it say this? It's teaching us that the Messiah will have the personal qualities and abilities of Moses as well as sharing the root of his soul.

Moses had a unique ability to recognize the true place of others, as shown in the verse, "Moses chose men... of all Israel and appointed them... leaders of thousands, leaders of hundreds, leaders of fifties, and leaders of tens" (Exodus 18:25). He knew how to assign people to their proper role based on the root of their soul. The Creator gave him this ability because he truly cared about each person and wanted to guide them to find their true place. He knew which people from the tribe of Levi should be musicians, which should be singers, which should be priests, and more.

This genuine concern and ability to recognize others' places made Moses the leader of his generation. And these qualities are what define every generation's true leader, the one who guides others to fulfill their roles and destinies through their God-given qualities and abilities.

The true leader is the one who guides Creation to its proper place, the place where everything is truly supposed to be according to the Creator's design. The Messiah will have this ability of Moses and every true leader of the generation. He will fulfill this role of helping others to find their true place on a global scale. He will help everyone to find a life path that is consistent with who they are, their positive natural tendencies, and abilities as discussed in Chapter 5.

The Soul of King David

The Embodiment of Personal Spiritual Growth

The second aspect the Messiah will have is a connection to the soul of King David. Many verses connect the Messiah to King David.

King David is juxtaposed with Moses in the aspect of the root of his Divine service. Moses was a man of the people—he unified the community and inspired them to love one another—while King David was the embodiment of personal spiritual growth. He spent much of his time and energy building and strengthening the inner connection of his soul with God and revealing the individual qualities and potential of the human soul to get closer and closer to the Creator.

It is also written that King David was the one to carve the path of repentance for the individual. In previous generations, repentance was a community affair. As we find with many stories in the Bible before the time of King David, it was entire communities, cities, or nations that repented after their communal inequity was exposed. In the days before King David, when the community turned together towards sin and was rebuked by a prophet or leader, they underwent public fasts and prayers and repented as a group.

King David was the first individual to repent to God and achieve forgiveness for his personal mistakes. In doing so, he revealed this possibility for the generations after him, that individual repentance was achievable. A person who has made a mistake can "own up to it," and once they sincerely return to a straight path and rededicate their hearts to the truth, their mistakes are forgiven and sins can be expunged at the soul level. This concept of personal repentance that was pioneered by King David also fits into the general aspect which he embodied, which was the individual's personal connection with the Creator.

This same dedication to individual inner growth will be embodied by the Messiah. In other words, he will bind the entire world together in one human family with bonds of love and respect, in the way of Moses, and he will also teach and inspire everyone to build a strong and palpable inner connection with the Creator on the individual level, in the way of King David.

In this way, the soul of the true Messiah will possess both these aspects of Moses and King David, both of which are needed to facilitate the true and Final Redemption.

How Will The Redemption Happen?

Redemption is a growing movement. As time progresses, we will see a larger and larger movement of people identifying with the Nation Israel, the Torah, and the Holy Land. Just as we see today, except with growing numbers, we will see the world shedding its foreign faiths and embracing the true teachings of faith with a unified and cohesive structure, without all the discrepancies of beliefs we see today because of the numerous false religions.

The world will recognize the true source of wisdom, and naturally be drawn towards it, while simultaneously shedding the false beliefs that clouded the light of their souls for so long.

Humanity will realize the need for mutual respect. We will know the importance of allowing space for others to be themselves. Peace will reign between all people. Jealousy will fade away and every person will be happy with their lot in life, and side by side they will realize their destinies.

When one realizes the importance of finding their true selves and expressing it in the world, they likewise realize the great importance of respecting the process of others doing the same. Their family, friends, loved ones, and neighbors also have their sacred mission, which is also key to the Creator's Master Plan. In understanding all this, every person will support those around them in finding their true destiny.

Today, people are lost in the world and slaves to fear because they're disconnected from their true identity. When you find your true identity, you find your true self and are able to go back to who you are. You return to your spiritual root and realize your true place in the Creator's Creation. This is the secret of repentance, to return to where your soul came from as you live your life in this world.

Depending on your soul's root, you have a certain destiny. Some people should live their lives by the sea, and others in the mountains. Some are meant to live in distant lands, and others in the Holy Land.

Every person has a soul-mission, a destiny, a place to inhabit, a perfect connection with the entirety of Creation, and more than that, their own key role in Creation.

ADDITIONAL INFORMATION

Procreation, Sparks of the Soul, God is With Us, The Sin of Adam and Eve, The Nature of Our Reality, The "Backend" of Creation, Spiritual DNA

PROCREATION AND THE SOUL

Soul Sparks: From the Man to the Woman to Their Child

When a husband and wife mate, sparks of the husband's soul are received by his wife. If their union results in pregnancy, the spark becomes a soul as the baby grows inside her.

As the baby grows inside the mother, sparks are added to the baby's soul-rope which determine their personality and traits. With great divine supervision, additional sparks are added that grow and expand the baby's soul and strengthen its connection above.

The child can also receive sparks though *Ibur* from the righteous souls of all generations. They come from the most known holy figures of the bible, as well as hidden righteous people whose names have long been forgotten. These sparks help the child and provide guidance throughout its life.

Sparks build the soul during the baby's time in its mother, after it is born, from the time of its bar/bat mitzvah, and during its entire life.

Sparks from the factors mentioned above, and more, are always interacting with our souls during our lives.

THE SPARKS OF OUR SOULS

Their Effect on Our Realities

The combination of soul and sparks within us is very complex, resulting in complications in our lives.

Some examples are in order:

Someone today can be a chef, greatly struggling with the decision to make their vocation their main income source, unsure if they'll be able to make ends meet doing so.

Immense challenges block the path to fulfill their souls destiny. Perhaps they're unable to find a job in a kosher restaurant, and contemplate pursuing their career in a non-kosher restaurant. Or perhaps they dream about opening a kosher eatery, but are unsure if consumer demand will be great enough to be successful. Their soul yearns to be a chef and prepare food, but their path feels so constricted.

They face their situation from an individual perspective, and they're unaware of the deep roots in their DNA that draw them to their vocation.

Behind the Scenes of Situations Similar to These Are Deep Spiritual Roots That Span the Breadth of Time

In the days of Moses when he met with the elders of the Israelite tribes, or in the days of King David and his son King Shlomo, when they would meet with their advisors, there was food at the tables upon which they sat. Chefs were grilling the meat they ate and preparing the dishes they dined on.

The person mentioned previously in our day and age who desires so strongly to be a chef, could be the direct ancestor of one of those chefs who cooked for the table of those great ones.

Furthermore, the chef who cooked for King David could have descended from a chef who also cooked for Moses, and today his descendant finds himself struggling to actualize the same passion in our modern era. Such hidden wonders are more than plausible in this world that is supervised so perfectly and fantastically.

Many Variables in our Lives Have Their Roots in Ancient Situations

These ancient causations are often hidden from our awareness, yet within life there are hints, spiritual remnants pointing to ancient pasts. Some people have a fantastic memory, a gift for arithmetic, or interpersonal relationships, while others have the complete opposite. These too are examples of variables in our lives with deep roots. Further examples can be easily imagined.

Even if someone is not related to major figures of our past, it does not mean that their ancestors did not number those who crossed through the deserts of Sinai and entered into the promised land. We are the continuation of them, and our lives are a continuation of theirs.

Conclusion

There are many wondrous systems of this Creation, and systems within each system. The concept of DNA and the character traits that are passed through the DNA is another aspect of the transfer of souls.

It is another system alongside the other systems of soul-transfer that carry the sparks of life through history and time.

GOD IS WITH US

People go through many struggles, both emotionally and physically. Many people walk the earth like empty shadows, disconnected from God and their own souls. Through it all, God is with us.

What Our Souls Are Made Of

Do you know what happens when you learn Torah? Even one letter learned with a holy intention counts as "learning Torah". It's written that the merit of learning Torah counts the same as fulfilling all 613 commandments of the Torah.

Even with such fantastic revelations of Divine grace, sadness and despair find a way in. A person can say, "But I'm not even Jewish! What good is the Torah I learn?"

To this, I say, so what? It's still written that you will be rewarded. The Talmud says that a non-Jewish person who learns Torah should be respected with the same honor due to the High-Priest of Israel. Therefore, never doubt for one moment, no matter who you are, that you will be rewarded for all the effort you make in this world.

Even small actions have great rewards. It's written that Abraham, our forefather, believed in God, and it was counted like charity (Genesis 15:6). Avraham simply believed in God, and his simple belief was considered as charity, which is one of the highest spiritual acts there are. Who is to say that the same thing can't be said about us? Our faith in God can also have far-reaching, spiritual effects. Our only problem is that we lack faith, we don't believe we are capable of such merits.

Many similar things are written that should change our perspective. For example, it's written that the world is sustained through Torah study, prayer, and acts of kindness. Yet still, even though it's written, we have a hard time believing it. When we sit and learn, do we feel the spiritual bounty being drawn to earth from heaven through our words? Do we have in mind that we are sustaining the world?

Most do not.

Despite our overall lack of confidence, holy actions do affect the world, and they do so greatly. Because of pure intentions, thoughts, desires, and actions, good things take place in the world. People find their soul-mates, weddings happen, couples conceive, communities receive livelihood, and more.

People who espouse such beliefs in our days are few and far between, even though these concepts are well documented in the holy books. Because such concepts are in fact written, most Torah believers would admit them to be true, but personally, there's a disconnect between these teachings and their perception of their actions. They don't connect with the concept that their simple deeds elevate spiritual sparks and bring blessing into the world in hidden and spiritual ways. If they claim to believe what's written, how come they don't connect personally with such ideas?

The Problem: Lack of Self-Esteem

We Don't Believe in Ourselves

Our lofty potential is limitless!

We may believe in a spiritual system of cause and effect, but we don't recognize OUR part in this system. This is a mistake that needs to be corrected — because the truth is, WE are connected to the realms above, and with every positive action, we cause the Creator's blessing and bounty to be brought into the world in an endless supply. We need to recognize our greatness and believe in ourselves, as this is a crucial part of our mission in this world.

Too often, we give in to the voices of negativity and self-criticism that plague our minds. We give our attention to everything that's wrong and imperfect with us, instead of believing in the reality of our lofty potential.

Many great things that happen are the direct outcome of our positive self-esteem and our belief in ourselves, and the incredible ability we have to change the world.

Our greatest potential and power is the ability we have to connect to our souls. We connect to our souls in order to draw blessings and bounty. We do this through prayer, kind deeds, Torah study, and many more acts, or even thoughts of devotion. We should be happy and proud of who we are, and believe in our ability to bring blessings to ourselves, our families, and to the world.

When we recognize our pure and innocent desire to connect to God beyond the limits of this world, we should be very satisfied with who we are. For this, our background or family tree does not matter, and it makes no difference whether we can trace our roots to known righteous families or not. Among holy souls, there are no souls that are better than others. It is only the illusions of this world that deceive us into thinking that we are inferior or superior to others.

In the eternal world, these classifications fall away, revealing the true reality, where only good and complete unity exist eternally.

In this world, we are not the only ones in exile, as God, the Creator Himself is also in exile. He clothed Himself within the world he created, and He is found within all levels of particles and life, including us. The forgetfulness we have to the spirituality of our souls is not only ours, it is also God's.

At the root of everything, including our souls, there is nothing except the Creator Himself.

THE SIN OF ADAM AND EVE

Its Spiritual Effect on Human History

When the Creator wanted to create Adam and Eve, He intended to project the highest light into a most noble creation. He wanted to make a creation that is complete like He is, with no need to mate or have any other physical needs.

However, at the moment He created them, Adam departed from this ideal and sought to fulfill his appetite for the physical world. The moment the Creator created Adam in all his holiness, clothed in light and holy shining skin, in all his glory and perfection, he immediately fell into the pursuit of lowly desires. He saw that the animals were created in partnerships of male and female, and he wanted this same relationship for himself. The Creator saw no other remedy and created Eve out of his side for him.

Adam and Eve loved each other deeply, but their descent from the heights of spirituality to the depths of physicality continued. Eve encountered the snake, and Adam reacted by mating with the forces of darkness. Through the generations succeeding them, Creation kept falling, level after level. Cain killed Abel, and humanity pursued a path of violence, rape, and all forms of deviation from the Creator's will. This has continued throughout history, up until, and including our current generation.

Amidst it all, the holy nature of our Creation remains present.

The Godly soul is always holy, no matter what it goes through. The Soul of Adam was shattered and scattered throughout the world. Although it was broken, its holiness remains present within its shards. Even though it went through much filth, disgrace, violations of Divine Law, and trauma, it is still holy. We are still holy.

There are two aspects with which we describe the Creator's relationship with our world:

They are:

The aspect the **Holy Blessed One**

and the aspect of the **Divine Presence**.

They are also considered masculine and feminine aspects, respectively.

From our perspective, the combined light of all men is the Holy Blessed One, and the combined light of all women is the Divine Presence. Still, within all men, there is a feminine aspect, and within all women, there is also a masculine aspect.

It's a beautiful teaching, but how does it fit into the harsh reality of the world we live in? What about all the rapists, molesters, wicked women, and terrible men? How does the teaching of the light of men and women coexist with the reality that our world is broken and far from perfect?

After the many destructions throughout history (the destruction of the Temple, the exiles, and more), it's written that the Creator became sad and angry. More allegorical texts describe how the Creator fell like a drunk man on the ground and that He fell into a deep sleep for 70 years. It's written that the Divine Presence screams "God curse me!" and refuses to receive consolation from her horrific pain. How can we understand what this means?

These statements describe characteristics of the Infinite One. By comparing the Creator with a man who reacts to his situation, we can grasp how the Creator, so to speak, reacts about worldly situations. But these emotions and reactions do not stay in a celestial realm, they have real world implications. Divine Anger brings violence, war, rape, mutilation, and all sorts of horrible things to the world. The tragic events of history are reflections of the Creator's anger and upset.

Everything that happens in this world is a Divine Reflection. It may be hard for many to accept, and harder for even more to accept personal responsibility as a part of the collective aspect of the Divine system. Yet, acceptance and responsibility is what we must actualize. We must truly return to God in all our ways, and that is the only thing to do.

Prayer, repentance, and charity are the only things that sweeten and cancel judgments of Divine Anger. It's the only thing we can do that will make a difference.

THE NATURE OF OUR REALITY

Thousands and thousands of people scream their lungs out in prayer to the Creator, searching for God. They live in locations around the world. The world seems to us like a physical place, but it's written, the "Spirit of God hovers upon the water." There are many kinds of water, both physical and spiritual. This world that seems so physical to us has many spiritual levels built within it.

Let's explore, try to understand, and believe in this possibility.

The Layer That Surrounds Creations

The Water

The Bible records that at the beginning of Creation, the world was initially covered entirely with water. The Creator made the large sea, and then all the water descended into the "depths." Only then was land revealed, and until today "the Spirit of God hovers upon the face of the waters."

This spirit we're talking about is like a crust, a spiritual layer that protects Creation. Every particle of Creation enjoys this spiritual protection.

Protective Coverings Within Nature

May Seem Purely Physical, but They are Forms of the Physical Manifestations of a Spiritual Principle

The atmosphere surrounds the earth and allows us to breathe. An egg is surrounded with a gentle membrane that protects it, and our brain is protected by our skulls. Fruits are protected with peels, and nuts with shells. These occurrences of protective coverings within nature may seem purely physical to the uninitiated, but they are forms of the physical manifestations of a spiritual principle.

These shells are not only protecting what's inside them physically, but they're also protecting them spiritually and energetically. They are an energy field that protects the inner essence of what resides within.

This Spirit of God protects us and surrounds us in every moment of our lives. When we breathe, we inhale this spirit. This simple understanding can be used as a great tool for meditation. Even the food we eat and drink, the words we speak, and the things we hear, are all interactions with the Divine, as this world is a physical reflection of it.

We can choose to live our lives oblivious, in a spiritual slumber, unaware of the miracle and Divine truth permeating our existence. Or, we can choose to "wake up" from the daydream of unawareness, and live our lives awake and aware of the truth, being that we are interfacing within the Creator at every moment.

The Path to God

Our Daily Lives and Everyday Experiences

The path to God is not to experience the entirety of His essence at once, this is impossible. Our path to connect with Him comes through our daily lives and everyday experiences.

Our daily lives are the interaction with the protective energetic covering that surrounds us, and by simple actions and even intentions, we can influence beyond our small realm of experience and comprehension.

When two people shake hands, they feel each other's grip. But at the molecular level, scientists explain they haven't even touched! Between the feeling of a handshake, at the smallest particle-levels, there is space. In fact, there is space between everything. Every particle in creation is isolated and contacts the particles around it. The energy field that surrounds them might be known by science by a certain name, but from a spiritual understanding, the spirit of God is what surrounds and protects every part of creation.

The Sapphire Stone

Separating the Levels of Creation and Spiritual Worlds

There is a layer that connects one spiritual world into the next. One of its names is the Sapphire Stone that is under God's Throne of Honor. It's described as being above the heads of the Holy Animals (who are angels) who carry the throne. Between the Holy Animals and God's Throne of Honor is the Sapphire Stone, which prevents the Holy Animals from touching the throne itself.

Layers separate the levels of creation like the membrane that separates the contents of an egg from its outer shell. Like the layer that separates an almond and its hard outer shell, or the membrane that separates between the brain and its skull, so too, a thin, subtle, spiritual membrane separates spiritual worlds.

Science also teaches that an electromagnetic field surrounds all matter. We can use these metaphors to understand the structure of the spiritual world.

The Qualities and Composition of the Spiritual Layers

God's Spirit of Love

What is the nature of the field that surrounds everything? We've described it as the Spirit of God, but how can it be further understood? It is the power of Love. God's Spirit of Love surrounds every detail of creation.

The Hebrew word for love, אהבה (*ahava*) begins with "א," the first letter in the Hebrew Alphabet. It is followed by "ה," a letter that is often used to represent the Creator, as in השם "HaShem," lit. "The Name (of God)." The third letter in אהבה is "ב," the second letter in the Hebrew Alphabet. The final letter is another "ה", the letter that represents God. From here, a pattern can be envisioned. After the final letter "ה" in אהבה, the third letter of the Alphabet can be added, followed again by "ה". The pattern can be continued to encompass the entire Hebrew Alphabet. Every letter of the Alphabet being separated by "ה", as in, "אהבהגהדההוהזהחהטהיהכה..."..... and on.

What Is the Message of This Pattern?

The Message Is That God's Love Is the Fabric of our Reality

The Zohar says, "He fills and surrounds all Creation". This is represented by the "ה" separating every letter of the Alphabet. The "ה" represents God, and the Alphabet represents the Creation.

For example, our skin is a layer of protection; it doesn't limit us. Instead, it lets us function in the world. So too, these spiritual shells allow us to interact with our surroundings. They are what let us smell, hear, taste, and exist in the world. Because this spiritual layer is the Spirit of God, the Spirit of God itself permeates all the talking, seeing, feeling, sensing parts of our existence.

It's written that the Creator created the world with His breath. There is a word in Hebrew, "*behebriatam*." It translates to "when things were Created." When this word appears in the Torah, the Hebrew letter Hay is written in a smaller size. The sages explain that this teaches us the Creator needed only to use a "small breath," represented with the small Hey, to create the world. It was no great effort for the Creator to create everything in existence.

Even Sapir - The Sapphire Stone

The Light of the Creator

This surrounding membrane between every particle of creation allows us to live, breathe and exist. This membrane is the love that binds all of creation together in unity and oneness. And this is known as the Sapphire Stone "*Even Sapir*" in Hebrew. In Hebrew, *Sapirit* translates as sapphire, but in English, *Sapirit* sounds like *spirit*. This hints the true nature of the Sapphire Stone; it is the light of the Creator.

Sapirit refers to the Spirit of God, the energy of love that separates God's Creation at all levels, from the smallest physical particle to the highest spiritual worlds. It heals and protects the inner life in every thing, shielding it from damage from external forces.

We need to know that we are blessed with this Godliness that protects us. When we fall into making mistakes in our weakest moments, and even if it feels like these mistakes dominate our lives, we should remember the verse "love covers all crimes." (Proverbs 10:12) The love that covers all creation, also covers the sins and harsh life experiences we have. The love soothes, heals, and corrects the damage from these difficult situations. For this, we should be very grateful.

Let's examine it honestly. In great kindness, the Creator blessed us with His love and mercy that surrounds us even at our weakest moments. His love is eternal and all-merciful. This Spirit of healing and support is the love of the Almighty Father to us, his children, the holy souls of the world.

On Redemption Day, These Secrets Will Be Known to All

When the redemption comes, and our spiritual eyes will be opened, we'll see how the Creator influenced our entire lives. We will see that our entire existence is only a reflection of the Creator's greatness.

Creation in all its aspects is a complete reflection of His greatness. The world is the most accurate reflection of His completion, with every specific level and unique aspect fitting together to reflect His completeness.

In the days of redemption, we will see that every moment is a particular reflection of the Infinite.

To all the broken, wounded, depressed, and traumatized souls, internalize the dictum, "there is a reward to your work." Don't be discouraged or fall into despair. Don't let the pain or challenges break you, instead let them purify you and remove the husks away from you. Hold on strong to who you are. Remember that you are an eternal soul that lives within a body. The real "you" is your soul. Your body is your chariot, your vehicle that lets your soul transport itself and function in this lowly world.

Our bodies are not who we are. Our souls are who we are, the life that lives within, the conscious and aware piece of God that's alive within our bodies. Just as God said, "I am who I am," we can also say this about ourselves. "We are who we are." Every one of us is a unique soul and within every one of us is a spiritual structure, a Tree of Life, and inner springs of spiritual "water" that emanate from within.

All holy souls are connected with an inner spiritual bond, invisible and unrealized in the physical world. We are unique but united and connected like a tree of life, everyone being branches of a huge tree that is a bloodline connecting all the holy souls. The deep spiritual realities within us are the spiritual springs and waters that connect us to each other and to our maker, the Creator of Heaven and Earth.

We should think about this and try to internalize this understanding. There is an outside layer of creation, what we see with our eyes, and this is what we interact with as we go about life, seeing, hearing, smelling, etc.

The Hidden Interactions In Everyday Life

However, there is a deeper, hidden aspect of life. These are the internal interactions we have with the external parts of life. For example, sights in the outside world travel through our pupils' holes and are understood by our brain. Similarly, smells waft into our bodies through our noses where our souls recognize it. These are examples of how external reality is brought within our internal realities, and this relationship represents a deeper, more hidden level to existence.

This relationship also works in the opposite direction, from internal to external. When we use the restroom to expel waste or blow our noses, energy is transferred from the internal to the external. Another example of this is when we cook food. When heat from the cooking evaporates the water within ingredients, the steam that results from it is a transfer of the food's inner essence to the external, in the form of steam released into the kitchen's atmosphere.

THE "BACKEND" OF CREATION

There are things we can see and are aware of, and there are many things in the world that we can't see and aren't aware of.

External and internal can alternatively be described as "revealed and hidden." There are many levels of understanding of this concept and many spiritual manifestations of this relationship. We will explain external and internal physicality and relationships found in the natural world, but the same concepts manifest in higher spiritual levels.

A Mitzvah Drags Another Mitzvah, and a Sin Drags Another Sin

Good actions cause good results in the world, and bad actions cause bad results in the world. Most of our actions have an inner (hidden) motivation. Our inner motivation is the reason why we choose to do one action or another.

For example, you see someone who looks like they're having a bad day. You wish to cheer them up. You give them a smile and a genuine compliment, or maybe some words of motivation. Your inner motivation was to cheer them up the reason you acted the way you acted.

But the influence of our actions do not stop when they are acted out. Our actions go on to cause an inner effect on some other part of creation. The sequence of influence starts in the inner/hidden realm, is brought to fruition the outer/revealed world, and then goes on to cause some other inner/hidden effect in the thing we interact with.

To continue from the most recent example, you said a kind word to someone who looked like they were having a bad day. Your words don't stop with them. No, they have a strong effect on the person who heard them. They were uplifted, and had some inner change from your sincere words of encouragement and kindness.

The Ideal Balance of Creation

The world is supposed to be spiritually balanced. For example, when you plant a tree, you plant it in soil. From there it grows.

The seed will grow in the soil from its inner/hidden potential. The hidden DNA and natural processes within it will cause a small seed to grow into a full tree complete with sweet fruit. We'll be able to see, touch, smell the tree and its fruit. But with our physical senses, we could never pierce the hidden essence of the seed to realize its innate potential that enabled it to grow into an entire tree.

When we influence goodness upon the world through positive action, the merits of those actions empower the spiritual structure of the world towards the side of good. To elaborate from the above example, when we say positive words to someone, the positive influence that emanates from us travels to the outside world and enters the ears of the one we say them, thereby making their way into his inner/hidden world. This way, the good is passed on. This process happens indirectly, like described above, and in more hidden ways. For example, the effects of good actions can positively influence people we've never met or known.

To continue our seed example, when we plant seeds of any plant, we're supposed to plant it in a healthy and proper place for the tree to grow. In the proper environment, the plant will yield good produce and grow healthy and strong, but in an improper environment, or if neglected, it will not grow well.

If we act negatively, for example, speak words of gossip and slander, or if we plant a plant in a field that's not ours, our negative actions will have a negative result. Even the fruits of the trees we plant in a field that's not ours will negatively affect the ones who consume the fruit. Because there was an aspect of stealing involved in the fruit's growth, there will be a negative aspect attached to it that will be passed onto the person who consumes it.

The creator created the world to function in an ideal way. There is a way it's supposed to work ideally, in its best version, like it was supposed to work in the Garden of Eden. There is also a "baseline," less-than-ideal functionality of the world that came to be its modus operandi after the sin of Adam and Eve. After these events, the world continued to function, but instead of being balanced, it functions through negativity and destruction.

Additional Information

When the world is fixed and balanced, running in its ideal way, it does not mean that it is completely clean from any negative aspects. Even if the world was functioning at its highest level, people would still have to use the restroom and blow their noses, the world would continue with its natural systems. Human existence would take place in a balanced way, meaning we would still experience those uncomfortable parts of life, but they would stay inside their proper boundaries without "leaching" outside their proper borders.

For example, the only thing meant to flow down the drains and sewers world flow down them, and nothing inappropriate or more than the basic requirements for the function of life would be wasted down the drains. Nothing more than the bare necessity would feed the "backend" of creation, which is the *Sitra Achra,* the Other Side/Dark Side of Creation that is hidden from us.

Ideally, when Creation is operating in its balanced state, the "Other Side" would be only fed its minimum requirement to upkeep its proper role in Creation. The waste from Creation that naturally exists would feed the bare minimum of vitality to the Other Side needed to sustain its existence, but no more. When God forbid the "Other Side" is nourished beyond its basic necessity of sustenance, its influence is empowered beyond its proper role. Needless bloodshed, spilling seed in vain, eating unkosher food, gossip, slander, angry outbursts are all examples of situations that cause the "backend" of Creation is being fed beyond its proper limit

The dark, hidden side gets more power than it's supposed to by these blemished actions. Through the extra "nourishment" it receives from these actions, the Other Side gains additional power to leach even more goodness from the world. The world is then influenced by the negativity and will cause even more situations where vitality is lost to the Other Side. This connects to the Mishnaic dictum, "On sin drags another one in its wake."

But it's also written, "A Mitzvah brings another Mitzvah in its wake." Just as negative mistakes cause more negativity, so do positive actions cause positive results to multiply.

The Lies That Cover the Truth

Ideally, truth is supposed to be always revealed and easily recognizable. But the lies in the world cover the truth with false claims of being the truth. The lies pretend to be the truth but are, in reality, completely false, "false truths." I'm sure we can all think of instances where people or groups claim unequivocally to be telling the truth but are completely lying in reality.

When a person does something good, the truth will come out of it. But when a person does something bad, lies will come out of it.

For example, if we do good and act justly, the energy that will influence the world will also be balanced and good. The truth would be recognized; it would be obvious and known to all that good actions cause good results. Everyone would be able to see this truth clearly. The positive results of our actions would be recognizable, and the blessing of good actions would be self-evident.

But when bad actions are done, lies cover the truth. The Other Side of the world receives, or takes, more energy than it should, and then it can create a false sense of reality that blocks the truth. In this scenario, lies have the power to masquerade as truth. Confusion reigns, and many are stuck "Calling evil good, and good evil" because the real truth is so difficult to recognize.

The Beard

For example, the verse says about Aharon, that when he was appointed to be the High Priest, Moshe anointed him with holy oil, and it came down upon his beard. The verse says, "As the good oil on the beard, the beard of Aaron, that comes down based on his (character) traits." This verse hints that the person's beard is meant to reflect their good attributes.

In the ideal state of Creation, if a man is good and his character is perfect, he should have a perfect beard. But if a man isn't perfect in his attributes and "trimming" his character traits, his imperfections should be visible in his beard.

The Torah describes God to have 13 Attributes of Kindness (Exodus 34:6–7). The Zohar describes "13 corrections of the beard" corresponding with God's 13 attributes of kindness. If a person possesses God's 13 Attributes of Kindness, his beard will reflect all 13 of his qualities of kindness. Accordingly, if a person is defective in his inner 13 Attributes of Kindness, his defects reflect on his beard. Literally, his beard would be less shiny or patchy in certain areas. This is how the world should work, but many times it doesn't.

These days, the world is imbalanced. The improper actions of humanity feed the world's backside with negative energy and lies, and the Other Side gets more energy than it's supposed to.

The Ways the Other Side is Fed

The negative side receives excess life force in many ways. Here are some examples.

-one throws out good food into the garbage

-someone wastes their money on negative and useless things

-a person gossips or says negative or destructive things

-when someone wastes their seed

-empty and pointless conversations

All these sins and empty actions give extra energy to the Other Side. With this extra energy, the Other Side has the power to masquerade as the truth. Through this power, someone undeserving is given a holy-looking beard even though they are evil and have no merit to carry a holy beard.

When the system is off-balanced, an evil person can now have a long, shiny, perfect, and full beard (a sign of good character). Another person will look at the beard of this undeserving person, and it will look like him like this person is righteous. The Evil Inclination does not let the truth be revealed and hides the truth about this person. Instead of his face revealing his rotten and evil character as it should, the extra energy in the domain of the Other Side makes this person look righteous. The truth is plastered with falsehood, and a shiny beard covers the face of an unworthy man.

A person who has an undeserving beard will confuse the world and attract followers. They will influence people to follow them because they will appear to be righteous and correct. But actually, they will lead their followers to dark places.

This is the way of the Other Side. It pretends to show goodness but pulls its victims into an evil trap. So be careful, don't follow "fake beards" and "false masks." Be positive and honest in your search, and may the Creator bless and guide you.

The main and only thing we have to do is try the best we can do good and avoid negativity. As simple as it sounds, there is not much more we should do!

Nowadays, everyone asks themselves, "Who am I? What am I doing here on Earth? " What's my purpose?" Those who go through life completely sure of the answers to these questions without pondering them deeply, in my opinion, possess a quality of arrogance.

A wise person is open-minded to learn from anyone, and not only from those who claim to teach. The Redemption that will take place will reveal the unconditional love the Creator has for all his children. Then we will finally understand the path to God and how God has led humanity from the first day of Creation until the time of Redemption.

There is something essential to understand about the concept of the Redemption. The Day of Redemption will be the day of the complete correction of the entire world. The Creator created the worlds according to the name "*Shadai*." *Shadai* is one of the holy names of God.

The sages explain the name Shadai corresponds to the *Midrashic* statement שאמר לעולמו די "*shemar leolamo dai*," meaning "He said to His world: stop." This dictum conveys that the Creator created the world with a limitation.

We know that the Creator is Eternal with no beginning or end. Logic might dictate that this world would also be Eternal, as the Creator is Infinite. But this is not the case. In this world that God created, He set limitations and boundaries, both in time and space.

Because of the limitations and borders in this world, people can exist. How could we live out our lives in a world where time and space were swallowed by infinity? We couldn't. Only through the limitations of time and space can we have a seemingly independent existence.

Everything always happens in the present moment, even though the present moment constantly shifts forward on the progressing timeline. This limitation of time is a feature of the name *Shadai*.

We experience Him under the limitation of time and place, but actually, all the moments are expressions of His infinite greatness. They're all happening simultaneously at a higher level, above the level of time. This is because above the limits of this world, there is no time.

We experience this world in limitations, but even this world is truly unlimited in a higher perspective. When one looks at this world from a micro standpoint, physicists admit they still don't know the smallest constituents of Creation. And also, on the macro scale, the universe is so giant, astronomers can only estimate its true extent. We see from these examples that this physical Creation is virtually unlimited in the furthest boundaries of existence and the micro and macro levels. Yes, even solid limits to physicality have yet to be limited.

Beauty that Reveals the Infinite

Endless beauty can be found in all systems of Creation and details of nature. The structures of particles, the layout of the planets and galaxies of the universe, and many more natural phenomena reveal the intimate wisdom of the Creator.

The Divine Supervision in life situations can also reveal the beauty and depth of the Creator. Small (or large) miracles connect situations and people together in perfectly orchestrated ways. Indeed we've all experienced times when we're thinking about a person and spontaneously run into them in the grocery store or receive text messages from them moments after they crossed our minds. All those amazing instances are tastes that reveal the Creator's perfect and precise supervision that governs our entire lives, not just those moments which are so evident.

All that we experience is meted out by the Creator's supervision, which gives us the portion of life we experience, and not more. For example, we are limited to time and space. We cannot experience any other time than the present moment, and we cannot be in two places at once. This is our perspective now. In the days of the Final Redemption, this will change.

SPIRITUAL DNA

Within the DNA of every person is a complete record and history of our ancestors. Modern science can only make general conclusions about a person's ancestry based on their DNA, but hidden within it is a precise record of their entire family tree. Every ancestor and who they were in their entirety is in the secrets of their progeny's DNA.

Today, most people around the world categorize themselves by nationality. They consider themselves Argentinian, Swiss, Ugandan, American, and so on. But many of the counties they claim have barely existed in the span of human history! The story of who we are is much more ancient.

Some people have a general sense of their family history going back for a couple of hundred years, but many don't even know this. Very few know a detailed account of their ancient roots.

A wave of forgetfulness sweeps over us that disconnects us from remembering the truth of our souls - who we are, where we came from, and what we all have in common. Our original roots are in the bodies of Adam and Eve.

Most see themselves as individuals who stand alone in the generation in which they live. Yes, they have brothers, sisters, parents, aunts, and uncles, but they don't view themselves as branches of an ancient family tree that they actually are. Although they might have close relationships with family members, they see themselves as individuals from their perspective.

There is no doubt that it is good and healthy to see ourselves as individuals, as it's true we are all Creations of the Creator with unique souls. But from a wider perspective, our individuality has a place within a rich and ancient family tree, the bigger picture of who we are.

We are units in a vast network of souls that spans across the timeline of human history. This perspective is something many of us rarely consider deeply, let alone incorporate it into the mindset of the way we view our lives.

Every generation sees itself as a new creation, a new human in a new generation. The ancient family history kept alive in our DNA is hidden from our awareness.

Through learning these principles, combined with inner contemplation and examination, we can find hints that reveal the ancient history found within us. Hints about our past are gleaned through our character and personality traits and other factors that will be described.

Adam and Eve

In our ancient most roots, we originate from Adam and Eve. Our souls and physical makeup were within them from the moment they were created. As they had children, the spiritual sparks that make up our souls were transferred to them. Their families multiplied through the successive generations, and tribes and clans formed across the face of the Earth, which became the great nations of antiquity.

The Forefathers of Israel

Twenty generations after Adam, Avraham was born. Avraham had a son, Isaac, and Isaac had a son Jacob. Jacob had twelve sons who became the heads of the tribes of Israel.

The descendants of these twelve tribes of Israel are scattered around the world. Some of us are surely from the Tribe of Judah, and others may have their roots in other tribes like Gad, Naftali, Yosef, and more. Our roots can be from multiple tribes, as families intermarried between tribes over many generations.

Forgetfulness

As we live our lives, we often face great struggles, too distracted to consider deeper spiritual sides of our reality. We are forgetful and unaware that our genetic makeup is the key to the deep secrets of our past and the blueprint of who we are.

If someone takes a DNA test that shows they have 3% Jewish DNA, it is only a vague hint at a person's ancestry. Current DNA tests are far from being detailed, and they can never tell the life stories of every one of our ancestors. Just because the tests can't tell the full story of every person in our family tree, it doesn't mean that they aren't there, preserved within us. These secrets of our past may be hidden from our eyes, but they're not hidden from the Creator, who knows our ancestral details in their entirety.

Remnants of our past are preserved within us and are within our grasp to recognize. These hints hide within our character traits, personality, and tendencies; they are remnants of our ancestors that have passed to us. Through internal investigation and personal observation, we see hints about our roots. Even if an expansive understanding is out of grasp for many, at the minimum, we can appreciate the deep history that shapes us.

Some examples will illustrate this concept further. Let's say a person has a spark from Rabbi Akiva's soul and also has a spark of the soul of our Matriarch Rachel. Even though this person is a man, he has feminine soul-sparks entrusted to him to elevate and correct.

Another person can have the character trait of rage which comes from the rage of Tziporah, the wife of Moses, while simultaneously having the character trait of peace, coming from Aharon, the High Priest. Both aspects can coexist within the person.

Someone else can have the sparks from both these souls, but their traits come from opposite sources, having the love of

Tziporah and the severity of Aharon. The qualities a person receives can be positive or negative, and they should be exercised as such by expressing the positive and working to rectify the negative.

The Stories of the Bible

Within the Bible are the records of significant events whose repercussions last many generations, and they also hint towards the roots of our inner traits. To understand our roots, we should believe in ourselves by believing we can recognize the connections we find between ourselves and the ancient biblical records.

Here's an example: Ten of the twelve tribes were lost and exiled from the Holy Land of Israel over two-thousand years ago. Although they moved locations, their inner character stayed the same, it's in their DNA.

Today, there can be communities in Afghanistan that are shepherds. Their society may be known to sell cattle and various kinds of livestock and has done so for generations. The real reason for this is that their DNA preserves their tendency towards this profession. Shepherding is not just something that happened to them by the circumstance, passed on out of convenience; there could be a spiritual reason for the tendency of their community to be associated with this way of life.

Their communities may be called "Sons of Yosef" (tribes in Afghanistan have this exact name). Their tribal name, in addition to their trade, preserves their ancient history. They are indeed the offspring of Yosef, and as Yosef was a shepherd, so are they. They would have a fondness for Yosef and share more of his personality traits. They would be kind, generous to the poor, and they might have a known gift for interpreting dreams as Yosef did. The ancient root of these tendencies may or may not be realized by them.

Additional Information

As another example, a tribe that descends from the Tribe of Shimon may be fierce warriors, known for their strength and courage in battle.

Looking at ourselves individually, we often don't see such shining and clear examples of heroism that would lead us to understand the precise spiritual root of our souls. Someone who proclaims such and offers precise conclusions about their ancient ancestry based on their character alone is probably not being realistic.

The qualities of our character are often subtle, and we feel like we have such drastic contradictions of traits that spiritual clarity about these topics seems very distant from us.

Through the thousands of years and many generations, families mixed extensively. People today can be from the tribe of Judah, from a certain clan, who married a family clan from the tribe of Efraim, and this took place two thousand years ago, with a long and complicated family history following. Many of us are intricate mixes of families, tribes, and clans that brought us here after thousands of years of complex history. The results are that every one of us draws from a unique spiritual origin.

The following is a series of transcripts of my public lectures and original teachings.

The Judgments of the Heavenly Court

The Creator creates the worlds. In the Talmud, the Creator is also called the Artist of the worlds, as there is a strong similarity between the words for "creator" and "painter" in the holy language of Hebrew. When you see beautiful scenery in Nature, you can easily understand Him being described as a painter.

Now, let's look at that description from a higher perspective. The Creator, "Who was, who is, and who will be," designed this world as an eternal one. Every moment that the masterpiece of Creation exists is an eternal moment. It is a masterpiece that spans from the ancient first generation to our current moment. And it continues on its timeline in our physical world.

Every angle of Creation is a picture, a snapshot in time. In every moment there is a situation, location, characters, objects, feelings, and much more. This is the story of each particle's life in this Creation.

In Heaven, there is a court that passes Judgment on every detail of Creation according to the Laws of the Torah. Therefore, we must not steal or lie. We must not covet, or commit adultery, or murder, or harbor anger. Instead, we must take care of others, help those who are in need, and do good things.

This Heavenly Court is responsible for the attribute of Judgment in the world, which is decreed according to the Torah's Laws. Every truly righteous man in every generation discusses the Laws of the Torah and interprets every word to ease the lives of humans and sweeten their Judgments. They do this to show the Creator that He must show mercy to His latest generation, the population of earth. This is the job of the truly righteous ones of every generation.

The righteous people are the mediators between the Creator and the Creations. On one hand, they favorably interpret the Torah and present a case to the Heavenly Court that justifies the generation as innocent according to the rules of the Torah. On the other hand, they rebuke the generation to wake their hearts to repentance so that they will stop sinning and reunite their hearts to the will of the Creator. This dual process of the mediator is personified through Moses. During the incident of the golden calf, he rebuked the Nation of Israel for their idolatrous practices, yet on the other hand, he defended and protected them from the Creator's retribution.

The Creator watches and reverses His Judgment, and works wonders and miracles for the ones who choose Him. The ones who choose Him are those who put effort into the tests of their lives. They choose their words carefully, work to purify their thoughts and desires, and have strong intentions with their prayers and goodwill. Their efforts pierce the Heavens. Every baby's cry and every good deed and thought of every person in the world also reaches Heaven. The Creator listens and sees everything, but earth's trial in the Heavenly Court continues.

The Final Judgment of Creation has not been finalized, meaning humanity is continually on trial. Every generation has its sages and its people and their opinions. Through their actions, they make good Judgments that ease and sweeten the trial.

In every generation, the Heavenly Courts are influenced by the actions of the generation for the positive or negative. So, who are the negative accusers in the Heavenly Court? Who are the ones who give power to the angels in the Heavenly Court to pass harsh Judgments?

Angels are also a Creation. They are the force that drives the physical and spiritual worlds. They are not Creations with free will like we are. They are refracting the light of Creation. They're the outcome of the decisions of the Heavenly Court—the force that executes Judgment, whatever it is. They are the result of the relationship between Eternity (*Netzach*) and

Foundation (*Yesod*). They are the manifestation of the first argument between the *Sephirot* of the Creator, in the way that the first light of Heaven came to earth.

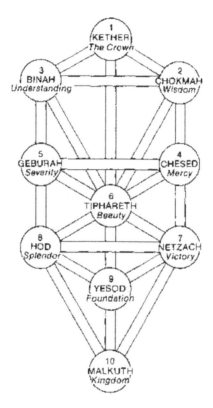

Diagram of the Ten Sephirot

As the light shifts, Eternity (*Netzach*) and Foundation (*Yesod*) are divided into a contradiction. Eternity does not stop as it goes on forever, and opposite to it is Foundation, which seeks to ground all existence. On the one hand of Eternity, there is no time or place at all; it's an unending movement of growth. But Foundation is the grounding force that creates the place for our existence. So they are opposing forces. Eternity seeks to move forward forever, while Foundation seeks to stay rooted.

The angels we're discussing are the outcome of that contradiction. They're the sparks of light that result from the contradiction between Eternity and Foundation. This contradiction also creates the *Sephirah* of Glory (*Hod*). The angels were given the Glory of Hod.

But the power to decide the Heavenly Court's rulings was not given to the Heavenly servants that we call angels. When a ruling from Heaven is issued, it must be reflected on earth, and angels are created as a result of the Judgment, to carry it out.

Light refracting though a prism

Just as light refracts through a prism to create a rainbow, so too the *Sephirah* of Foundation is the prism that refracts and establishes our physical world. As soon as the *Sephirah* of Foundation refracts the light from Eternity, it creates the world, which has free will, desire, and all sorts of hiding places.

When the Heavenly Court makes a decision, it creates the refraction of Eternity through *Yesod*. This is the Creation of the world. The decree itself creates the physical world because it is the refracted light.

This world is a clean and perfect reflection of the Divine Judgment of the Heavenly Court, and everything that goes on in the world is a reflection of the Court. Every detail and situation that occurs in the world, both outside of us and also within, is only a reflection of His wisdom and His teachings, and the Judgments that are based in the Torah.

And remember that every moment of life is a stand-alone eternal snapshot. Every moment is an eternal snapshot which is the result of the Judgments of the entirety of Creation since the beginning of existence. That culmination of existence is judged and created in every moment by the refraction of light of Eternity through Foundation.

Every moment of Creation can be compared to a rainbow refracting light through a prism. In Creation, there is an exact number of everything, such as trees, doors, boys, girls, and even all the words said in every conversation. Every word, thought, and action of Creation is recorded; all of Creation's records are written down and carved, which make the entirety of history.

The angels are the engine that runs the world. But someone gives life to all Creation behind the scenes, and that is the Creator. He is the one who supervises everything that is happening in the world. But the Heavenly Court decides the decrees which are carried out on earth.

In the Heavenly Court, there are two sides of people who try to influence the Judgments either to the good or bad, to the right or the left, to the side of mercy or that of harsh Judgment. Some raise criticism and have bad things to say about humanity, and some expound the merits and goodness of the world.

The ones who judge favorably and learn the Torah beautifully are righteous. The righteous explain and teach the Torah as the revelation of the Creator's mercy. They see the goodness in the heart of humanity and daily they teach the people on earth that there exists true good, and they inspire them to stop sinning and to search for the Creator.

By the work of these righteous people, Creation is healed and the souls of the world get stronger. They give power to the angels to sweeten all Judgments with mercy, but only when the Heavenly Court accepts their claims. They find favorable Judgments according to the Torah for every individual and the Creation as a whole. By doing so, these righteous people nullify dark Judgments and break the judgmental people who are responsible for creating them.

When people engage in Torah study, their words are being examined in Heaven for their validity. When righteous people judge favorably and learn Torah in the aspect of revealing kindness, they bring grace before the Heavenly Court.

But who gives the validity and authority to the angels that bring harsh Judgments in the world? Who is responsible for the punishments that come down to earth? These are the leaders of lies who study the Torah while they are wrapped in personal mistakes. They ask for Judgments and turn people evil through their teachings. Through their twisted Torah study, their mouths speak horrible decrees that bring suffering and pain into the world. They do not judge people favorably—on the contrary, they speak negatively about people and misinterpret the words of the Torah.

They learn the Torah in a twisted way, as if it's full of Judgments, anger, rage, frustration, and darkness. Therefore they judge negatively and decree with their mouths, "These people should die, these people deserve to suffer and be punished," and so on. But those Judgments do not fall on the individuals they target; instead, the entire Creation is judged altogether, and the Judgments fall on it as a whole.

The Creation is on trial as a collective unit, based on the collective outcome of its actions and history, as discussed above. The true reality is much greater than our personal perspectives, and the things that happen in our lives are the results of the trial in Heaven between good and evil.

The good, righteous ones cleanse and purify. And the brazen, cowardly, and judgmental leaders argue, ridicule, and disagree with the righteous leaders of truth who work to reveal the Creator's true will to show mercy and bring abundant goodness to Creation.

The evil people whose minds are twisted and hearts are filled with anger, frustration, and fear, judge everyone as if they also are evil. They assume everyone is as cowardly, twisted, selfish, and evil as they. This is why they argue and fight with everyone. The Holy Torah was given into the hands of people to use and interpret, but because they are not worthy to use it and possess so many evil qualities, their Torah interpretations damage and destroy the worlds in many ways.

This is why the Torah fell to earth, the original Tablets were broken, prophecy ceased, every person isolates themselves with their fears, and most people forget their personal connection with the Creator. This is how the world has fallen into distraction and lack of consciousness.

But the trial in Heaven continues between the righteous leaders and those who are wrapped in mistakes.

Every good thing we do rises to the scales of Heaven and represents the side of good. And if someone does something wrong, their actions bear their guilt and strengthen the side that opposes good.

In the future, the claims of the Messiah will finalize the trial in Heaven. The Messiah will be known as *Mashiach*. In the holy language of Hebrew, *Mashiach* is spelled the same way as *Mesiach*, which means "conversation." As in the Hebrew phrase משיח ליבו עם בוראו meaning, "Conversing with his Creator." In other words, the Messiah will have the power of speech. He will pray his heart out to the Creator in prayer and his Torah learning and conversations with friends and students will present good claims to the Creator that will be accepted by the Heavenly Court.

The Messiah will say only righteous things, and the righteous path will shine through him, and the light of goodness will be revealed to those who follow him. The claims that come from his mouth will reach the Heavenly Court, and through those sweetened and favorable Judgments, all the souls of the world will receive healing and abundant goodness. He will find the right claims to show Heaven that it is correct to only judge Creation favorably and positively.

The trial will then be finalized and the present time will rise and shift to a level of redemption. In that moment of the Final Redemption, every moment since the beginning of Creation will be uplifted and transformed. It will be the elevation and salvation of every particle of Creation, not only in the present moment but throughout all time. The span of human history will be elevated and redeemed. Every trial in the Heavenly Court throughout time will also be redeemed, and every harsh Judgment will be reversed.

When the Messiah explains and teaches his approach, the Creator will rule the Final Judgment following his holy words. He will judge that it's time to redeem the world.

This debate in Heaven started thousands of years ago and is still happening today, but the Messiah will bring the trial to conclusion with his final speech.

And in the future when that Final Judgment occurs, all Creation will shine. Not only will the Messiah's generation experience the light, but every moment of Creation since its beginning will experience a holy ripple effect, and have healing and Completion. Then redemption will occur across the timeline of human history. Every second of the painting of God will be redeemed. All the points of time that existed during history will be included and experience redemption, in the moments themselves.

Everything will become connected, and depending on the level of perfection we have reached, we will connect with all the moments along the timeline in a bond of loving unity. Every aspect of Creation through time and space will be influenced and uplifted by the righteous side of the Heavenly Court who defends the Foundation.

This Complete Redemption is dependent on us and the Correction of our character traits.

Therefore, everyone who is holy in their heart and carries within them the light of goodness that existed from before time and Creation should pray to the Creator, "Holy One, I am thankful that you gave me the privilege to experience You through the temporal world, but I refuse to be judged by the courts of false leaders who destroy thousands of souls and worlds every moment by their evil speech. I want only You to judge me with your mercy and by the wisdom of your righteous Messiah."

Who Am I?

I am the person who sits, experiences, and hears the struggle of my soul. My soul seeks to express itself and see the Creator express His love for His children whom He made.

But, opposite the power of the soul, an evil obstacle exists. It looks through our eyes and sees a physical reflection of infinity in the shape of our world, and it brings our souls to destruction by being consumed with the illusion of physicality that surrounds us. Like a spice that adds flavor to food, the evil inclination changes a person's experience in life from good to bad.

The word for "soul" in Hebrew is נשמה, *Neshama*. Because the soul faces these struggles and obstacles, the Creator gave us a lifeline, the Oral Torah. The Oral Torah is the wisdom of the soul. It is the *Mishnah*, spelled משנה, the same Hebrew letters as for *Neshama*.

There is a great soul Correction in learning Mishnah. It gives the soul the power to shine the light of the Torah, teaches us how to differentiate between right and wrong, and fuels our soul in the battle of free choice. It gives us the power to choose good over bad, based not on self-interest but rather on eternal faith, trust, inner goodness, and honesty.

It is the struggle of all human beings, both as individuals and as the general public (as a united soul), to see good and not evil in themselves and others as well, and to always use free choice to seek out this good.

Our success depends on our thoughts, actions, and speech. We experience the world around us as a direct outcome of our choices, because the combination of all thoughts, actions, and speech of all human beings brings into being the reality that surrounds us. It is a rule of Nature in this Creation, and it applies always.

According to our point of view and our unique position at the threshold between good and evil, we are the designers of our life and the entire world. For that, we must do good and improve our character, for ourselves and for the world's Complete Redemption. It depends on us, as a group and as individuals. Everyone should think specifically about themselves in regards to this issue and dedicate themselves to stable growth and not to destruction

The Importance of Holiness and Purity: How to Fix Ancient Mistakes

Certain explanations are needed to grasp the practical advice in this lesson. This lesson is not easy to give, and it's not taught happily. Rather, it's with a lot of thought that this topic is breached, as it's a very sensitive one. In fact, the only reason we bring up such topics is the great and important lessons to learn from them.

The souls of Adam and Eve are the same soul we have inside of us today. The only difference is that theirs is divided among all humanity. Souls get weaker though the generations, and every new generation cannot contain as much soul as the previous. Because each generation can only fix as much of their soul as they can, the uncompleted sparks of soul go to the next generation.

It's well known by almost all people in the world that Adam and Eve sinned. What is less known is that their failure has still not been fixed yet, and it's our job to complete it. Everyone knows they failed by eating the forbidden fruit. There was a big problem in their relationship, and the actual events which took place at that time are not widely known. It can be very sensitive and uncomfortable to learn, but it is something we must face.

Think of one huge body, broken down to billions of pieces. Adam and Eve's soul is fractured into those billions of pieces, and every one of us is in charge of one of those pieces. Those pieces are our souls. We are each in charge of what we were given and, to the best of our ability, must finish its Correction. By taking responsibility and putting work and effort to Correct ourselves in the right way, we will cause an awakening for others to do the same. We can cause a giant movement and revolution to sweep the world.

Let's take the next text we are about to discuss and turn it into a practical lesson. Most English speakers who have read the Bible do not know of the deep rabbinic tradition that surrounds and explains all of its texts. They are unaware of the Oral Torah, the true transmission of the Divine Torah given to the Nation of Israel and preserved through thousands of years by the Jewish sages. We can never know what happened or understand the true intentions and depth of the verses just by reading them as they are written in the Bible.

The Holy commentator, Rashi, explains that when Adam arrived in the Garden of Eden he was surrounded by animals. In his sudden manifestation as a physical being, he was overcome by physical desires and urges. Rashi explains that as soon as Adam awoke in the Garden, he began to mate with all the animals. Adam was a very holy and pure soul, but he was never taught the Torah. He had no teachers or previous experience and never learned the right way to behave, and he was simply overcome with the sexual desire that was a result of his newfound physicality.

He mated with all the animals but was not satisfied, so he complained to the Creator that he could not find a suitable partner. The Creator then made Eve. Immediately Adam mated with her, as it is written, "Adam knew his wife, Eve." Again, we see the strong desire of the man for sexual fulfillment.

After their union, Eve wandered in the Garden and saw the Snake. The Snake saw Adam and Eve mating earlier and the Snake desired her. A very uncomfortable reflection is that the Snake most likely raped her as he was trying to persuade her to eat the forbidden fruit. We know this because it's written that the Snake contaminated her, and since then, the offspring of man and woman have been contaminated with the contamination of the Snake. We are talking about physical contamination that exists in the seed and has existed within the offspring of Adam and Eve since her encounter with the Snake.

It's man's tendency to blame the Snake. We always ask ourselves why the Creator created the world to have the Snake in it. We put all of the blame on the Snake for the horrible events that happened as a result of the Sin. But the truth is that we were the problem, not the Snake.

Adam failed. His problem was that the first thing he did when he came to earth was to mate with the animals, and after he couldn't find satisfaction with them, he asked the Creator to make Eve. He immediately mated with her as well.

Something is very off track when you think about this story, especially considering how the animals were made in those days. In those days, animals came to the world as pairs, as described in the verses of the Bible regarding Noah. Every animal was created as a male and female pair, and together they were a couple. In the days of the Bible and especially in the first days of Creation, things were very simple, innocent, and pure, or were supposed to be. Every animal had its mate and they were a simple happy couple.

If Adam found himself having relationships with the animals, it means that he split up the couples and took a mate away from its true partner. Because he did this, he opened the door for the Snake to do the same with his wife, Eve. If the Snake had never witnessed Adam sleeping with all the animals' partners, it would have never crossed his mind that he could do the same with Eve. It's only through Adam's behavior that the Snake learned he could do the same.

This is something we must take responsibility to fix. But how can we do this? How can we regret or take responsibility for something that happened such a long time ago, even though we are part of Adam's soul? The Creator wants us to understand the outcome of that mistake is still carved on our spirits. Our current mindsets and the general state of humanity still reflect the results of Adam and Eve's choices. Adam's passions lead him to sleep with the animals, and Eve also allowed herself to mate with the Snake.

It reflects in our minds today. Even though we aren't (God forbid) sleeping with animals, sexual perversion still exists in our minds. We still have thoughts of lust and desire for things we have no business to desire at all. We must realize that Adam and Eve's ancient mistakes are still implanted in us and we must take responsibility for it by working on and fixing the perversion that exists within us.

A great truth and inner working of the spiritual system that runs earth is that we are all responsible for the things that exist in the world because all souls are connected. We can see, with great sorrow, that human trafficking, child predators, and all sorts of horrible perversions and crimes are still taking place. Even if we are not engaged or involved with those things in the slightest, we must examine our connection to them.

The souls of the world are dependent on each other. Even a person who is very pure and almost always far from forbidden or lustful thoughts can examine their role and connection to the darker side of humanity. For a soul like this, their mistakes can be very slight, such as not being sensitive enough to their loved ones or not being kind enough. When a spiritually strong person on whom many souls depend makes even slight mistakes such as those mentioned above, it can bring darkness into the spiritual channels they're connected to and lead others to much worse mistakes.

Every person should take full responsibility to guarantee the souls they're connected to by being the best they can. Souls are responsible for one another because all souls are of one unit. If your soul is on a higher level in the structure of souls, it means that those who are attached to you are influenced by you both positively and negatively. If you experience some sort of positive growth, so too will that blessing flow to them. They might feel a stronger desire to come closer to God, or something similar. So too, if someone on a high level makes a mistake—even if it is relatively small—because they are who they are, it causes darkness to pass through to those they are connected to, and those may experience much worse mistakes, God forbid.

We should never desire things that don't belong to us. We should never desire a man or a woman who doesn't belong to us. We should never look to the sides and gaze at their figures, and if you see something that sparks your desires, guard yourself and divert your mind to another direction. Never feed your lusts by watching filthy things online or the like. It's very important to take an active approach and take these things very seriously.

People are so sensitive; they will immediately look at themselves and blame themselves for their shortcomings. They will think about all the times they failed in these things. But this is not the lesson we should learn. The lesson is simply to understand how the system of the world works and decide today to walk on the straight path.

Never fall to self-blame and self-hatred for your past. It's a waste of time and energy. The main thing to do is just to learn what we should do from today onward and do the best we can. We should guard ourselves against the foreign desires mentioned above and do our best to be nice, sensitive, and good to our loved ones and those around us.

Millions of people have addictions to lust. It's horrible to know that so many people are caught in these traps that take the love and passion out of marriages and damage so many souls. When I see these people struggling, I want to help. It's very important and necessary to understand that if you violate the rules of the Torah, you're doing something bad and the outcome of your actions will be harmful to others.

How do you recognize if you're doing something wrong? A person may think their actions only affect themselves. They might think that even if they see and watch things they're not supposed to, it won't affect anyone around them. But here is the test: If they're lying, they're wrong. If you're lying to or hiding things from your loved ones, you're violating the Torah and you're in the wrong. A liar can never stand in front of the Creator, and a group of liars can never accept the face of the Divine Presence.

If you realize you are lying and hiding and you want to change and fix, the first step is to take responsibility. The first step is *not* to lay out all your junk to your loved ones. Spilling and confessing years of your sins and crimes to your loved ones will only kill them emotionally. Only if you give them, starting today, years and years of happiness to make up for all the pain and emptiness you created, should you bring yourself to confess. Only after creating abundant positive emotional padding with years of true friendship and happy delight, can they handle a confession as you might have.

There is no higher pleasure than to know you're making others happy. One who constantly seeks satisfaction will never be truly satisfied. But when you change your intention to become one who desires to satisfy others, you can have true inner wholeness and satisfaction.

When you put effort into fixing the defects in your mind and spirit as we discussed, you're completing your part of the grand picture of Creation that was given to you to complete. The souls that are connected to you will also enjoy and develop in similar ways. Everyone will be upgraded. May the Creator assist us in all His ways. Amen.

How to Understand The Creator

You can learn about the Creator through learning about yourself, for we were made in His image and likeness.

We all have our inner personalities as well as our external behaviors. There is the inner "you" and the "you" that you show to the world; your true self and your behavior.

Each of us is aware that our external actions are not always aligned with our inner selves. Acts of rage and anger can be traced to feelings, such as of innocent love and desire to be loved, that were unmet. A lack of self-confidence can cause us to invest our love and attention in the wrong places.

This disconnect between our true feelings and emotions and our external actions is a reflection of the Kingship of Heaven. This is also known as God's supervision in the world.

The Creator has His own "personality," which is pure goodness and includes the Thirteen Attributes of Mercy. The Creator also has His external actions, which comprise the Divine Supervision of the world along with its "Judgments," the bad things that happen on earth.

These harsh Judgments are not the true will of the Creator's inner being. They are not expressions of who He really is, but rather the results of the Judgments calculated by the system of the Heavenly Court, the system the Creator made to judge the world according to its actions and intentions.

When you understand this teaching deeply about yourself, you will be able to penetrate through the layers of the Creator's Divine Supervision and recognize His true goodness. This is the inner aspect of all Creation and the Creator Himself.

The practical action we can take from this understanding is to invest more effort into revealing a true correlation between our true inner selves and our external actions that is based on goodness. Doing so gives power to the Kingship of Heaven to overpower the system of Judgments in place today. This allows the revelation of Divine Supervision over the world that is based on His true inner goodness and infinite kindness.

Miracles in Our Days

There are many miracle stories told about our holy ancestors. Moses split the sea, for one. Righteous people pulled down miracles as the result of their prayers. There are many miraculous stories about women too; it's written that Sarah, our Mother, would light candles for Shabbat that would stay lit from Friday evening until Friday morning of the next week.

Many of us today find it easy to believe in the miracles of the past yet find it difficult to believe that miracles can take place in our generation. We might think it's due to the lowliness of the generation that miracles don't happen anymore.

The truth is, if you lived in the generation of the Baal Shem Tov, you would also find it hard to believe in the stories you would hear about him. Even if you lived in those days, it would be much easier to be connected to the wonders of the past instead of the potential of the present.

The evil inclination has no problem in us believing in past miracles and wonders; his problem is us to believing in ourselves. When you "wake up" to walk the path of the righteous ones, the evil inclination wakes up with you. He puts effort into thwarting your beliefs and stunting your devotions by making you doubt yourself and your ability to be answered and assisted by the Creator.

People in our generation are indeed making miracles and wonders today. There are those who are dedicating their hearts to the Creator in prayer, and in turn, He is revealing His kindness to them. And they are bringing down blessings and bounty to the world.

The truth is, we cannot believe in the Creator without believing in ourselves. We must believe in our ability to walk the path of the righteous ones just as was possible in earlier days. The evil inclination doesn't want us to do that, and he tries with all his power to make us doubt our spiritual potential.

We must also realize that no one is exempt from trials and tribulations. David, the Eternal King of Israel, had a life filled with torment and obstacles. Moses was separated from his family for extended periods of time. Joseph spent twelve years in prison with nothing except his faith to hold him steady. Righteous people of every single generation since the beginning of Creation have suffered and experienced difficulties. The difficulties we go through are part of life; they don't mean we are failing on our paths or being punished from Above.

When you look at yourself, you will always find yourself limited. You don't realize the expanse of your spiritual reach and the positive influence you have on others. Your power is enormous. When you praise the Creator, thank a person, or express the talents of your soul, you're influencing much more than you realize. We should believe in our talents, pursue them, and believe with complete faith in the Heavenly results of our good efforts.

How to Face Impossible Situations

What should we do when life tears us down?

Sometimes we face extreme challenges where opposing parties pull us in different directions. Examples can be our spouse versus our children, our parents versus our dreams and goals, our goals versus our life obligations, religion versus our families, and many more.

People can find themselves stuck in very difficult situations due to such conflicts, and many houses have been broken as a result.

I want to share something that I learned from my relationship with my wife. She and I never gave up on each other, regardless of the pressures we were facing or the forces pulling us apart. We never gave up our continued conversation and dedication to our relationship. My wife put in a lot of effort, and so did I.

But we as individuals must not allow our own commitment and effort to depend on that of our partners. The main responsibility we should take is for ourselves and our own effort. The commitment of the individual to the best that they can do is critically important. This commitment must not be dependent on the partner (meaning that we only try our best if they do the same).

It's easy to divide the obligations of the house between spouses. We can think, "I will do A, B, and C, and they will do E, F, and G." It may seem like a simple and logical solution, but in reality, things are often not so simple.

If your partner seems to be slacking, you should ask yourself why. You should investigate in depth why, in your opinion, your partner is not pulling their side of the relationship. One of the first things you should remember is that your spouse is a soul. They might be facing anxieties and pressures they haven't expressed to you. Maybe they have had trauma that you haven't, or maybe they suffer from low self-esteem to a greater degree than you do.

You might find your partner has many reasons for their behavior and difficulty. The possible situations and conflicts are so numerous and varied that it's impossible to cover all of them here in detail, but my main advice is simple: Have faith in your relationship.

The spiritual development that springs from the effort we put into fostering a relationship based on love, dedication, honesty, and respect is immense. It cannot be put into words. So as long as there is hope, even if the challenges are great, we should take responsibility to do the best we can.

The Creator sent us to this world for a period of time, for a mission. Even though this world is physical, our mission is spiritual.

The world that we see with our eyes is not the big picture of Creation. We don't see God's Plan. Rebbe Nachman says that when we judge another person favorably, we put a "good smell" into them. This "good smell" gives them a fresh breath that brings them to repent and come back to the Creator.

We don't always know what is going on with our partners, but we should try to understand them. They may be distant because they are worried, or rude because they are frustrated, and so on. I do not support abusive relationships at all, but it is undeniable that people find themselves in very difficult situations.

A parent might be very oppressive to their child who wants to pursue their dreams, trying to force them into the future they want for them.

Another person might find that their obligations to their religion separate them from their partner and family. These can also create horrible pressure and tension.

The approach I propose for any conflict involving people close to us is as I discussed earlier—that we should take responsibility to do our best despite the forces that oppose us. We should stay true to ourselves and our dreams and obligations while having sensitivity to the other party. When we take that approach, in time we will see the spiritual results.

May we have much success and help from Heaven in all our difficult situations, and abundant blessing from our sincere efforts.

"Oh God, Create Within Me a Pure Heart"

There can be many situations that push us to call on our Father in Heaven. People can experience such challenges and difficulties, and face such inner despair and confusion, that they see their only option left is to call on the Creator in personal prayer.

In a perfect world, we would run daily with a happy heart and wishing soul to have a conversation with the Creator. But we see very clearly in our lives and the lives of others that too often times of desperation bring us to call on Him.

In times like these, whatever brings us to talk to the Creator (even if it is goodwill and desire to connect with Him, or at least a belief that the personal conversation is important), we can find it very difficult to pray. We can feel like we don't have any sincere words, or after five minutes of speaking about everything we had on our agenda, we can feel empty of inspiration or motivation to continue talking to Him.

Whatever the specific situation may be, words can be hard to find and speak. But there are a few teachings and advice that will prove very effective in pushing through those barriers that block us from praying properly.

The first thing to know is that personal prayer can be an aspect of Divine Spirit (*Ruach HaKodesh*, in the Holy Language). Many simple and ordinary people who practice personal prayer regularly can attest that their prayers sometimes "flow" in a special way. They can find themselves answering their own questions through the unfolding of their speech.

For example, they might ask the Creator, "Help me have peace with my spouse. Help me respect them more and be sensitive to their feelings and emotions." There! By not even realizing what they were saying, their prayers hinted at them where they should work to get the results they need. First, they prayed, "Help me have peace with my spouse." Then they were immediately answered through their next words, "Help me respect them and be more sensitive..." The Creator led them to answer their own prayer. The answer to having peace is to respect and be more sensitive. This concept can be experienced easily and frequently by those who put effort into personal prayer.

One request will lead to another. Your words will flow, and through that, you will gain deeper insight and understanding. That is a real aspect of Divine Spirit and the Creator's guidance and supervision expressed within your personal prayer.

Before the standing prayer in Judaism, we say, "Lord, open my mouth..." (*HaShem sefatei teftach...*) This is teaching us that prayers come from the Creator Himself. He is the one who opens our mouths, and the prayer that comes through our mouths is actually from Him. That Divine Spirit is coming through us and expressing itself through us. You may ask, what is needed to have those prayers that are in the aspect of Divine Spirit?

You just need to go to a quiet place as free from distractions as possible and do it. Literally! Just do it.

You can go to personal prayer with your heart open, full of joy and happiness, or you can go as a result of struggle and pain— as long as you end up there and are willing to give it your best effort.

When a person isn't happy and prays out of desperation, they need to put a lot of effort into "starting their engines." They need to push themselves to express themselves properly.

One way to push yourself is to simply force yourself to talk. Even if you don't have a fiery passion and you don't feel like it's honest or sincere, you just force yourself to talk. With hardly any feeling, you can just push forward. In that way, one word will take you to the next until you can express your heart, your true inner emotions, and your good desires, and pray properly.

Alternatively, a person may find themselves empty of things to say. This person can plan to spend one hour in the personal prayer, but after five minutes, they find they finished their prayer, having talked about everything they wanted to.

In this scenario, you can look deeper for a point of honesty that is connected to your present moment. Ask yourself: "What's going on with me? How do I feel now?" Maybe you will find a lot of desires sitting in your heart or mind. Maybe you will speak about the fact that you don't feel you have any words left to say.

Another method to stimulate prayer when it's difficult is to sing. Rebbe Nachman says that when prayer is in song, it's like a beautiful queen wearing beautiful garments in front of the king. The king would not be able to stop himself from answering all the queen's requests because of her beauty.

You can sing known tunes in the realm of holiness or even songs you know from the world. Sing to the Creator those simple songs and know they are loved and appreciated.

Speaking to the Creator as you would to your best friend means that everything you expect to be able to tell and reveal to a best friend, you can to Him.

The most innocent, simple, and naive prayer is the highest of them all and is the prayer that will be answered.

There's a verse in the Bible that says, "God, create within me a pure heart, and renew within me a correct spirit." (*Lev tahor bara li Elohim...*) When we say that verse, the intention is to ask the Creator to purify our hearts and spirits to be able to stand before him, and to pray and express ourselves to Him properly.

In conclusion, many of us find these teachings inspiring but find it difficult to take into action even if we try. The answer is simple, we just need to do it. May the Creator surely bless, help, and assist you on this journey.

A Conversation with The Creator

I tell you the word of the Creator: "I speak to you all as equals, I am the infinite one you came out from. We designed this world together, but suddenly you left us and went down into it. I have been calling you again and again since then, but only now at this moment can you answer. In the present, I am calling you to come back and to focus on Me. I am asking you to think only about Me. Now. Only focus on Me, as I do on you. I am asking you to stop chasing the world we created."

One asks in response: "Don't you realize and understand that I have been thrown into this dark pit with no knowledge on how to find my way out or how to get back to where I came out from?"

The Creator replies: "Know, my son, that you shall not die. You will live a longer life than anyone has known before. All the blessings of my true love will go to you, and it will show you how far my goodness goes. You all are dear to Me, and I choose to see you as My brothers. I choose you to be part of the Final Redemption. To be united with Me as one who feels like he is sitting among his siblings as equals. To you, my promise is reserved."

The Creator is talking to us from a perspective above the level we are stuck under. We are being asked by Him to climb above the largest challenges we are facing in our lives. For us, those challenges are hard hours of darkness and despair. Those are the same hours we are begging Him to take away from us. We don't know how to solve our problems, so how can we be judged and doomed because of a challenge we undertook unsuccessfully?

The Creator knows our thoughts and says: "My child, I never left you. It is all coming to perfection; all the separations are coming back to one. We both are reaching out to each other, and it is all about to match."

Having Faith in Our Positive Influence

Every person fills their natural role in humanity. Someone who likes to dance *must* dance. They will never know how deep and powerful their dance is.

We often criticize ourselves and think our actions are only great if they're praised by people, but this is false. When we realize our actions are connected to the spiritual world, we also realize that our spontaneous desires to act are given to us because of a spiritual reason. We realize it is the Godly will that we fulfill those desires—even simple things like making a cup of coffee or singing along with a song that's playing.

A person who sings can elevate and empower worlds in a spiritual way. They can accomplish this even just by singing when they're completely alone.

We already know that the effects of our physical actions are beyond our perception. We can give a smile to a person that can bring up their mood and enhance their day, and as a result of that positive momentum they can go on to make a positive decision that alters their life positively forever. That is an example of a simple, easy-to-do physical action whose true reach and effect we have no way of tracing.

The same principle is true in the spiritual aspect.

When we watch an inspiring class online, our perception of the success of that class is based merely on the likes and comments on the video. We have no way of perceiving the full impact of the class. It is likely that people who watch that inspiring class take some advice from it, bringing its positive effect into their lives and even the lives of others. Through the ones who see that class, its light can be passed to others who haven't seen it.

The same effect occurs in the spiritual world through our actions—when we say a blessing over food, or when we follow the desires of our hearts to dance or sing. When we sit and learn the holy authentic sources of knowledge and wisdom, the Creator brings blessing into the world beyond the spectrum of our perception. We need to have faith in that.

Our obligation to believe in the Creator is beyond our ability to "see" and perceive His Godliness. We must believe in the spiritual reach of good actions and intentions even though we cannot perceive their true effects.

Our faith must be greater than our ability to perceive. We must have faith in ourselves to simply express the good within us and have faith that the Creator made us unique individuals with special characteristics and abilities for an important reason.

Why Your Prayers Aren't Being Answered—Serving the Creator with All Your Heart

How can it be that we are praying prayers to the Creator over and over again that go unanswered? How can it be that the one who controls Nature, the one who is above and in all situations, is not answering us?

The main thing we are lacking is heart. We must serve the Creator with our hearts, and then all of our prayers will be accepted and answered. We learn this from the universal proclamation of faith, the *Shema*. This is most commonly described as prayer, which is called "Service of the Heart." There are two explanations on how to serve the Creator with all our heart through prayer. We must emphasize that what we are discussing is most effectively practiced in personal prayer—the personal conversation between the person and the Creator that is so vital for spiritual growth and development.

The first explanation is that prayer should be spoken with power, strength, and vitality. You should pray with attention and focus on the Creator of the world.

The second explanation, which is our main focus today, is that a person should pray with an honest heart—a heart that has both positive and negative emotions. We must bring into our prayers *all* of our heart, whether we hold anger, depression, sadness, jealousy, or any other negative emotions. They too must be expressed before the Creator during the hour in which we pray. When we fail to do this, we lack a simple honesty that is needed in order for the Creator to reveal His true mercy on us and answer all of our prayers.

The Creator is abundant. He is the one who controls all situations and lives inside of all souls. He is the one who is giving us the personal prayers that we pray, and He is the one source of our positive and negative emotions. So we must express ourselves completely and disclose and divulge all of our hearts, all of our feelings in our personal prayer.

In this generation, we suffer from an extreme lack of self-esteem. We are extremely judgmental about ourselves and others in an illogical and harmful way. It can be that we disregard someone simply because they look different from us. This is a level of the spiritual contamination of death, *Tumat Met*, of this generation. We mentally "kill" people for no reason and with no end. We must solve these issues in our prayer and purify our minds and our hearts.

But the only way is to face these issues honestly, repent for them, learn the correct way to think, and allow the Creator to open and purify our hearts. Once we realize our faults, we must take the next step in the repentance process. If we only recognize our faults, we can easily fall into sadness about our current situation and never take the step towards actual purification and Correction of our negative character traits.

You might think that the next logical step is to promise ourselves never to sin again, never to fall into Judgments, never to fall into anger or any other negative attributes ever again. But, in reality, this would be a lie. It is an impossible mission to never fall again and to turn our backs on all our negative attributes. The real, honest, and only true option we have is to dedicate ourselves to working on our faults and to making an effort to do better in those areas where we recognize that improvement and healing are needed. We should try to avoid anger as much as we can, to always cheer ourselves up from sadness and depression, and to always connect to the positive attribute that is opposite to every negative one that we find within ourselves.

To try is better than to promise, and is a more realistic setup for success.

When we sin, darkness is created. Darkness in our lives and darkness in the world. It creates husks and coverings (*Klipot*) that conceal the true goodness of the Creator. When we dedicate ourselves to working on our faults, we remove these darknesses from all aspects of our lives. By realizing faults and dedicating ourselves to working on them, we allow the Creator to shine his kindness into our lives and consequently into the world.

Another fault we can fall into is to sin against ourselves. Low self-esteem, self-harm, self-destruction, and self-neglect are all sins that greatly harm us spiritually, emotionally, and mentally. If you feel you have fallen into such sins, you must identify your problems, issues, and mistakes. You must apologize to yourself. You must be kind to yourself and realize that the Creator wants you to be kind to yourself.

Many people who picked up religion from dark pasts have fallen into this mistake. They have lost themselves in an extremely complicated set of rules and guidelines which they are constantly pressuring themselves into following strictly, and then falling to self-hatred and sadness when failing in any one of these religious guidelines. They have lost themselves, and instead of working on their inner issues, they focus on a hollow aspect of the religion and ignore their inner worlds completely.

A person who pursues real inner repentance will be dedicated to the inner truth we are discussing. They will be brave to face their issues, faults, and failures, and they will not hesitate to discuss them in front of the Creator and make a positive resolution to work on themselves. When they fail in their character traits, they will not fall to sadness; instead they will look at all the times they are succeeding and most of all rejoice in their goodwill to improve. It is important to focus on this goodwill to improve and not fall to sadness whenever you fail. If you have the goodwill to improve, you are already succeeding!

The most important part of repentance is for us to be truthful and honest with ourselves. When we are truthful and honest with ourselves, we begin to build self-esteem and become more willing to give ourselves another chance. God is merciful and desires for sinners even of the worst kind—murderers, the worst you can imagine—to repent sincerely and walk in a straight way, connected to and desiring Him. Can you imagine a greater kindness than this? God's mercy is literally endless, and you should never fall to self-hatred because of anything you have done. You should simply realize that you made a mistake, then take your issues and discuss them in front of the Creator.

The moment you connect to the truth with all your heart, all gates of mercy and compassion from Heaven open. Your prayers will be answered and you will see miracles and wonders in life.

It takes patience and determination. As long as you are still making up excuses for not being fully honest, you cannot succeed. As long as you are falling to sadness and choosing to stick to your ways of negativity, you cannot succeed. But, the truth is that the Creator is waiting at every turn for you to return to Him in complete honesty.

At every crossroad and every turn, the Creator desires your entire heart, both the good and the bad. When you work on being honest with yourself and stop hiding the things you need to work on, you will find Him in every area of your life. You will remember that He is directly present in all situations. You will realize the people you are talking to, the situations that come your way, are all designed and planned by the Creator, and that He is within all aspects of your life.

In order to come to these beautiful places and understandings, you must "purchase" this truth. You can never truly realize these things from reading an article or even learning from the Holiest of Books. They must be purchased through work and dedication. This is an inner search that leads to an inner existence.

When you lie to yourself, you will never recognize lies in the outside world. Once you clarify the truth within yourself time and time again, you will be able to recognize the truth both in the outside world and from within your being. Lies will not confuse you anymore; you will be able to spot them from a mile away.

The way to achieve all of what we have discussed is through simple and honest personal prayers. If you wish to serve the Creator with all your heart and have your prayers answered and accepted, you must take time every day to have a personal conversation with the Creator and with yourself. Have an honest discussion out loud. Real prayer is expressing your thoughts and emotions in words and speech. Thinking is not enough. There are many very deep and mystical concepts associated with spoken prayer; it is essential that your prayer is spoken out loud.

May your prayers flow abundantly and honestly, and may the Creator give you the words to express your whole heart—the good and the bad, all that you need to work on. May it be easy, relaxing, and a revealing process. Dedicate yourself to living a life of truth. May all your honest prayers be answered and accepted, and may you be blessed by the King of all Kings.

The True Nature of the Creator

The true nature of the Creator is mostly hidden and unknown to us. For centuries organized religious institutions have forced their followers into a system of rules and obligations connected to reward and punishment. They have led their followers to believe that the Creator's influence is on our lives externally. Let us seek to carve deeper and reveal an additional aspect of the Creator which shows how He is connected with our lives.

Our most ancient teachings discussing the Creation of the world reveal deep understandings about the Creator and how he operates and exists within the Creation.

Upon the Creation of the world, the Creator "hid" Himself in every part of it. Why is He described as hiding? It is because he is largely unknown by his Creation, which is us.

The Creator disguised Himself in our world. He has access to and is witnessing through every set of eyes in human beings, animals, and insects. He feels every feeling of those creatures and experiences every moment of their lives.

The Creator is infinite and above time; His experience of this world is not limited to time. Therefore He is experiencing the entire timeline of Creation in his present, infinite moment. He lives the entire life of every generation and every individual in His perpetual present.

All of the joy, happiness, and satisfaction as well as all of the horrible suffering, pain, and torment that has taken place since the beginning of Creation is being experienced in the present moment by the Creator.

He lives inside of us. His infinite wisdom, compassion, and all other good qualities are locked inside of us. We are mostly unaware of His presence, but He is with us. He looks through our eyes at the sights we see, He feels the feelings we feel, and He shares the thoughts we have. For Him, it is a prison. He is tied to the tips of our minds.

Imagine for a moment how our Creator, whose true nature is pure benevolence, is forced to witness and experience his Creations kill, torture, rape, and extort each other. He lives as the slaughterer and the slaughtered, the bully and the bullied, the guilty and the innocent.

For Him, it is a disaster.

A majority of our world is living low-caliber lives mostly involved in fulfilling self-interest. We chase pleasure, money, and other self-centered desires. But in our consciousness lie the keys to attain redemption for ourselves and the Creator who resides within us.

With our self-awareness, we can connect to the Creator's presence within us. The secret lies in our thoughts and feelings. We need to recognize the lies and falsehood that plague our minds—the thoughts that lie to us in order to lead us away from being ourselves. We need to no longer allow the lie to live inside us, and instead only be honest and sincere.

It is unbelievably simple: Our good thoughts come from our souls, the spark of the Creator within us.

Have you ever felt wholesomely well, happy, or blissfully content? These are minute experiences of the Creator's true essence that we can experience. That inner goodness treasured within us, the Creator's presence, is the warmth of our souls.

We must reveal the kindness of the Creator within ourselves and aid others in doing the same. By strengthening our inner connection to the Creator, we give Him the power to express

Himself more within us and likewise through others. Our bodies are separated, but our souls are one.

Through self-awareness and talking out loud to the Creator, we verbalize His goodwill treasured within us. Through verbal conversation, we free our minds from obstructions and fears and come to positive and stable conclusions about our true desires in life.

This conversation between a person and his Creator is a tried and tested method. Rebbe Nachman of Breslov said that all the true righteous people of previous generations who arrived at true knowledge of the Divine achieved these things through the simple method of personal conversation with the Creator.

The key is honest and straightforward speech. The Creator is closer to us than we can imagine, and He is not obscured from the clouds of nonsense that fill our minds. He knows us better than we know ourselves, and He is with us.

The only way to truly connect to Him is to talk to Him openly, as one would to a best friend.

One person's prayer might be: "Dear Creator, please hear me. Please reveal yourself to me. I have always believed but never known what exactly to believe in. I have been searching for the truth all my life but have never found definitive answers. I simply want the truth. I simply want to connect with you. Please answer my prayers."

Another person might say: "Dear God, please assist me. I have made many mistakes in life that I truly regret. I have been searching for a way to change my ways but at times it seems so hard and impossible. I have fallen many times. I am desperate for a solution. Please help me."

Every person's prayer is unique, and only we as individuals have the power to pray our prayers to the Creator.

When we pray our prayers and dig deep within ourselves to express the emotions and desires hidden within us, we forge a connection and strengthen the Creator.

You may be wondering if you read that right. *Strengthen* the Creator? Yes. That is exactly what we do when we pray to Him with an honest heart.

As we mentioned previously, the Creator is installed inside of us and all of Creation. The way His greatness is revealed is through people.

While it is true that there have been righteous people throughout the generations who have taken it upon themselves to strengthen the Kingdom of Heaven, one looks around at the state of the world and it is desperately obvious that much more needs to be done.

The culmination of Creation is the Final Redemption. In the Final Redemption, the Divine spark within us will be fully revealed, and a spiritual shift beyond the current reality will occur. The world will be shifted to a higher existence.

Our work today is to reveal that Godly spark, our soul, the Creator's presence within us, as much as we can. By personal conversation and building ourselves, we create sturdy vessels that allow us to "water" those around us and spread the inner search and expansion of consciousness.

In the Talmud, it says the highest form of wisdom is kindness. On a simple and practical level, people's lives can be changed and even sparked to the purpose of life from a simple positive interaction. A simple conversation or even a few words in the proper measure can spark the soul of an honest person to seek the truth.

We must be aware of our surroundings and ourselves, and we must operate in the world as a soul surrounded by souls, on a mission to free our higher selves, which is the Completion of all souls.

By being an honest and sincere person, we inspire others to do the same. There are enough fakers in the world in all parts of life. It is our mission to be real. By being simple and real, we inspire others to do the same. Honesty and sincerity will lead others one way or another to the ultimate truth: that there is no existence except through the Creator.

Time, Space, and the Final Redemption

This moment in time is a moment that is eternal in all its aspects. For example, now, you're sitting where you are, reading this, with your thoughts and life experience, surrounded by all the details of your life. Everything around you, including you, has its roots in an ancient time and place. Everything has its roots in the ancient existence that was before Creation.

Explaining it is simple. You're sitting where you are, let's say, in front of a table. But that table was not always a table. Before it was a table, it was a tree. Before it was a tree, it was a seed in its parent tree. On and on, that tree's origin and indeed all existence has its beginning in the Garden of Eden, where Creation originated.

Every particle in existence has an ancient root in a spiritual place beyond time, in the original thought of the Creator's mind. As it's written, "The Creator looked into the Torah and created the world." *(Bereishit Rabbah 1)* This is why we call the Creator "the Place." We call Him this because all the aspects of physical Creation originated in Him and also because every moment is a reflection of the Creator's name *Havaya*.

At this moment, you have physical Creation surrounding you; every person is in their surroundings. All these details are the details of the Creator Himself. Meaning, it's Him Himself behind a curtain and filter of physicality. All the aspects of physical Creation—their history, function, purpose, and so on—everything in the "Place" is a reflection of the Creator Himself. All this relates to the name *Havaya*.

Havaya means the present moment. The highest way we know the Creator is the name YKVK, which we learned is not allowed to be pronounced out loud. Every part of our physical world is actually above time because the name *Havaya* (YKVK), which is the present moment, is likewise the name of the Creator in the highest way we know Him.

As is known in science, every physical thing at the molecular level is not solid. It's a system of different elements and atoms that are, at their root, vibrating energy. When one solid thing touches another, to our eyes it looks like there is a clear separation between the objects; but at the particle level, everything is interacting and exchanging energy. Creation itself shows us that every detail is not isolated and that everything is connected.

A phone is not just a phone. It's used to communicate, work, teach, and perform other functions. A tree can be turned into everything from tissue paper to furniture, which can be used by a person sitting at their table using the phone mentioned above. All of the details in Creation are attached to each other and attached to this grand "Place" of Creation.

From this understanding, we can stop looking at ourselves as isolated individuals. We are part of a greater interconnected picture which is an eternal existence.

Everything in Creation is not just a simple physical thing, it is a concept. For example, an apple is not just an apple. It is a certain variety of apple, planted in a certain geographical area, part of a species that is one of the thousands of strands of apples which have existed and developed for thousands of years.

Time can be broken into moments. Yet, every moment is a slice of time that exists in its eternal purpose. Each moment is a manifestation of the Creator's will. Every single moment had its history, circumstance, and components which led it to be manifested exactly as it was, all according to the Creator's will.

Everything we experience now is perceived through an extremely thick barrier of physicality. But if you envision it with a higher purpose, you will see everything is flowing in an eternal masterpiece of perfect interaction and connectivity. Much can be explained regarding the intricacies which are the variables that make every moment that perfect manifestation of the Creator's will.

There is a court in Heaven that reveals to us the Judgments of the Torah, the book of rules that was given to the hands of the righteous scholars. The words of those scholars—and even ours, when we are judging situations—are lifted to Heaven and presented in the Heavenly Court as evidence. All of our conclusions are adding to the scale, and the moment of our present time is a conclusion of that moment's conclusion.

As we speak (not only *when* we speak), Judgments are being brought down from Heaven. When we speak positively, positive things are taking place in the world; when we speak in judgmental ways, the same reflection is being brought to the world. It's not our fault, it's simply the simultaneous relationship that exists between Heaven and earth.

To understand this, we must "go out of ourselves" and our self-centered mindsets to understand we are all connected, and the reflection of the Judgments that cover the world are a sum total of the billions of lives, situations, and interactions that occur in every moment. We are not directly responsible for the outcomes of our lives. The outcomes of our lives are supervised based on billions of different factors and Judgments that we are not consciously aware of, and the effects of our lives also reflect onto others' lives—even others whom we have never spoken to and are not aware of.

The Creator gave the Torah to the sages to judge the world. As soon as the tables were broken by Moses, the Torah came to earth and the ability to affect the Judgments of the Heavenly Court was given into the hands of people.

The Creator listens to all sides of the arguments. He listens to the ones who judge and criticize in a harsh way, as well as the righteous ones who judge favorably with kindness and mercy.

And also every prayer and good intention ascends to the Creator and is heard Above.

The numerical value of eighty-six is, in Gematria, "Nature" as well as *Elohim* in the holy language of Hebrew. The Creator uses the name *Elohim* to run the world through Nature. That is the name that brings out the fruits from the ground during their seasons as well as all the bounty on earth.

But on the day of Redemption, the name *Havaya* will have complete authority. As of now, the reason Judgments are able to come into the world is that the name *Elohim*, by default, runs Creation.

The righteous ones lead the world through the name *Havaya*. They lead the world through His aspect of kindness, and they know the Creator's main quality is "Father of Mercy" as the eternal now, and that He's not only a strict judge. By judging others in a positive way and interpreting the verses in a way that draws people closer to the Creator through kindness, they fulfill the Creator's true will. They don't use the Torah as a weapon to fight, manipulate, and scare people. When the righteous overpower harsh Judgments with kindness, the name *Elohim* is replaced with the name *Havaya* and the supervision of the world is based on kindness and endless generosity.

On the day of Redemption, "All Israel will be friends." Everyone who was ever connected to Israel will be friends. All the offspring from the twelve tribes and everyone who contains within them a single spark of the goodness of Israel will be friends. Every one of the seventy nations who wish to serve the Creator will humbly accept the leadership of the Creator under the supervision of the name *Havaya*. The ones from the nations who are too stubborn and unwilling to accept the supervision under the name of *Havaya* will find themselves stuck in the old Judgments of *Elohim*, and will not be part of the future.

In the Redemption, all the timeline of history will be accessible to us as an experience. Since the Redemption will be above

Nature, it will also be above time. All moments will join together and we will be able to experience all the past time zones at once. That is what it means to be "above time." It means we will be able to travel in time and experience Creation in all its aspects and see the Creator and understand all His understandings.

This is the true explanation of the Resurrection of the Dead. We will be connected to everything that took place in every moment of time. We will see all the people from the past, and they will be able to see you. You'll be able to watch and experience Creation from all angles throughout history.

The illusion of the world will be broken. All truth will be exposed and true goodwill be known in every way.

The Creation will be run by the name of *Havaya* according to His endless kindness, and not through the system of Judgments as it is in our days.

In every moment we will see complete justice. All evil will melt into the earth's flaming core and will be the flame that feeds the warmth of the earth for a thousand years of peace.

If you see yourself as evil in any of your ways, it's the time, my brother or sister and friend, to work on yourself so as to not be evil in any of your ways anymore. Fix yourself to be as righteous and good-hearted as you can and only express your good nature. Banish all that is evil within you, that none of your limbs will sink to the fire on Redemption Day, that you may come perfectly complete to the Final Redemption. Amen.

The Redemption Will Come Through the Internet

The Lubavitcher Rebbe was first told about the internet after it had begun to gain popularity. When he was informed about what it is and how it works, he had one thing to say: "The *Mashiach* will come through the internet!"

The internet is the primary way in which the world communicates and is connected today. Billions of people are using a handful of social media outlets to share their lives and connect with others.

While a surface-level examination of the internet and social media will lead one to believe that it's mostly mundane interactions and expressions of people, the Lubavitcher Rebbe in his holy foresight saw a much deeper purpose.

There is much filth that passes through these channels of communication. People use it to communicate hateful ideas and speech, boost their selfish image, and channel their lusts and base desires. But the true purpose of these channels will be connected to holiness and purity.

Think of it this way. If the Creator were to create a road, many people would take advantage of it. Criminals might use it as a getaway route after robbing a bank. An abusive husband might use it every day as he travels to and from work. But the Creator does not appreciate those people using his road, even though He created it and allows them to use it.

The true delight of the Creator is when His Creation is used by righteous people to do righteous things. A righteous man who travels to give a lecture could be the entire purpose of the existence of that road. To carry the wisdom of the Creator.

From this metaphor of the road's true purpose, we can also realize the purpose of the world.

The purpose of the world is to reveal the Creator. The nature of the world is that it hides the Creator's existence, meaning that from our perspective His existence and supervision are not revealed for all eyes to see. The Creator allows mundane activities and even unpleasantness to take place in the world in order to preserve His hiddenness. Therefore the purpose of everything in the world and the world itself are not known to all.

This will all change when the Final Redemption comes. From the time of Redemption, everyone will know the entire purpose of the world and everything in it is to reveal the Creator.

This brings us back to the true purpose of the internet and social media. If we realize that the purpose of the entire world and everything in it is to reveal the Creator, so too would that include all online media and outlets.

It simply means that the internet is a way for people to connect to the wisdom that improves their lives and their inner connection to the Creator. It is a resource for education and connection to bring people to their personal redemption.

Every soul has a different mission and responsibility in life. One soul may be responsible for freeing itself from sadness, while another soul must work on anger. Millions of people around the world need life-saving and soul-watering content that is distributed on social media by honest people working for the good of humanity and the sake of the Creator.

Some people have a hard time waking up in the morning because of the pressures of life. Others face extreme social anxiety to the point where going grocery shopping is a daunting task.

These are suffering souls who need a spiritual remedy. Their remedy comes through the internet. Through inspiring videos that teach them about positive self-esteem and the beauty of their souls, they begin to heal and shift for the good. This brings us to practical and vital advice about *Mashiach* and the Final Redemption coming through the internet.

While we dream up wonderful fantasies such as live-streaming the Temple being rebuilt for all to see, we have yet not reached that point upon the publication of this book. Those who are working for that day have more to do.

We have the powerful tools of social media at our fingertips. We are not only privileged but also responsible for using it for a good purpose—the ultimate purpose. Social media gives us the ability to reach hundreds, thousands, and in some cases even more people with relative ease. We have a responsibility to be a positive stream of influence on these channels and to promote the search for truth. Whether sharing original posts and content or those of another who inspires you, you can try to reach those souls who need the light the most.

At the click of a fingertip, we can share an inspiring video about faith to hundreds and thousands of our friends and followers. The light of the Creator can be brought through these channels of social media to heal and wake the souls of those who are suffering in painful and often unknown exile.

Someone who has never thought seriously about the purpose of the world can be educated on the truth in five minutes! Someone suffering from depression can learn wisdom that can change their lives completely. Someone who formerly scorned the idea of the Creator can now find an explanation that fits and satisfies their soul.

It's all in our hands. It's up to us to be channels for the Creator to reach his beloved ones. By deciding to post, share, and reach out to those in our circles, we are providing the light to others and using the internet for its true purpose.

The world will indeed be healed and will prepare itself for the Final Redemption through the tools and outlets available to us.

The Mission of the Final Generation

There is a Heavenly voice that calls daily from Heaven to earth. It is the voice of an angel that teaches the Torah anew each day. Every person must qualify themselves through cleansing and purification for their soul to receive the light of the Torah that comes through this voice. Those chosen ones can listen and receive the Divine of the Creator.

Every time a person begins to learn Torah, they need to prepare to learn it as if they were standing on Mt. Sinai to receive the Torah like our ancestors. The modern-day descendants of the tribes of Israel are not just the Jewish people.

The Jewish people are only one of the twelve tribes of the Nation of Israel. Ten of the twelve tribes were exiled, and today their descendants are scattered among the nations of the world. They will all be included in the Final Redemption and reunited with the Jewish people. The Nation of Israel will be one again.

It will be very difficult for Jewish people to accept their lost brethren. Suddenly, they will be surrounded by spiritual giants, powerful souls on the same spiritual level as them and in some cases greater. The only difference between them is the exiled souls of Israel were lost and disconnected from the Torah, while their Jewish brethren sacrificed for generations to preserve its holy Laws and teachings.

However, when the spirit of *Mashiach* cleanses the earth and cleanses us of all negative character traits, we will not harbor any envy or jealousy towards each other. Rather, we will unite in love and respect to pursue our common mission to work for the world's ultimate harmony—being able to live in perfect peace with all mankind, with resources for everyone, and of course understanding our spiritual nature and connection with the Creator.

The challenge is to remember the qualifications that allowed our ancestors to receive the Torah on Mt. Sinai. They were a humble, united nation who were following the righteous leader of their generation, Moses. They were a nation that together was like one man with one heart and soul, aimed at fulfilling the Divine will and keeping the Laws of the Creator. By that incredible and paramount unity in purity and holiness, they were able to merit the supernatural revelation of the Torah, which is described as the Creator revealing Himself to them.

When we compare that lofty and noble level that our nation held in the ancient days to where we stand today, it is no surprise we are unable to hear the voice of Heaven that has continued to emanate to the earth.

Even though we feel disconnected to those ancient days, we must not think that the Creator has abandoned us, even though compared to the previous generations His supervision has appeared to have lifted. In reality, He has been with us continually since the ancient days.

We see that in all generations there have existed certain righteous and holy individuals who have led their fellow truth-seekers of their generations down the path of true Divine service. These righteous leaders have left us books explaining their understandings that continue to light our way until today.

Many of us have also felt the hand of Divine Providence guiding our lives in one way or the other—whether it has assisted us, taught us valuable lessons, or simply reminded us that we are in the care of the Creator, as if He winked or waved at us to remind us that He is with us.

All these leaders, holy books, and personal experiences are the Creator's supervision over us. He is with us just as He was in the ancient days when we experienced public miracles and revelations.

The only difference today lies within our distracted and disconnected hearts and minds. The state of the world today has put this generation in spiritual darkness, leaving the public largely unaware of and detached from the Creator's presence.

From the Creator's perspective, He gives the same amount of supervision and guidance on us as He did in the ancient days. The only difference is that, in His wisdom, He decided to send humanity through a period of decreasing spirituality and increasing darkness until the Final Redemption takes place.

Our mission, as part of this current generation of the Divinely ordained exiles, is simply to hold on to our faith in His Plan. Even though we cannot see and experience the Creator's presence as our ancestors could, we must hold on to our belief in Him and in the Final Redemption. Even if we don't see results from our internal and external efforts to purify ourselves to get close to Him or to improve the lives of ourselves and others, we must continue through the darkness; and when we do, we will ultimately witness the Redemption ourselves, with healthy eyes.

◆ ◆ ◆

ABOUT THE AUTHOR

Born to a secular family in Jerusalem in 1978, Rav Dror Moshe Cassouto began to return to the path of Judaism in his late teens and early twenties. He studied in several well-known Torah Institutions in Jerusalem before finding his extended residence in a well-known center under the banner of Breslov Chassidim. He was greatly influenced by the teachings of Rebbe Nachman and spent the next twelve years at the institution learning Torah and walking the path taught by Rebbe Nachman with great devotion and extraordinary effort. He was made the director of the institution's English department, where he began uploading his classes online; it was then that his lectures began to gain attention from a much wider audience.

Several years later, he left his position to form his organization, the Emunah Project Inc. Under his directorship, the Emunah Project Inc. carries out his mission of sharing faith and Torah-based education with the world through many projects, productions, and outlets.

People from all walks of life and backgrounds credit Rav Dror with helping them to make fundamental improvements in their life. The testimonials are unique and quite varied, but the recurring theme in the majority is that Rav Dror has shared a great light with many thousands of souls struggling with various forms of darkness. His deep teachings have provided a catalyst for spiritual seekers' growth, and his practical advice has helped many others live life more in tune and actualized with their authentic selves. His understandable and easy-to-understand explanations of the Torah's hidden secrets reveal his intimate understanding of the topics. However, his main effort is always dedicated to reaching out to others and sharing wisdom to help honest people's lives in whatever place they're in.

Today, the main work of the Emunah Project revolves around producing and distributing Rav Dror's teachings in various media forms as well as communicating with the many individuals from around the world who reach out with questions. With Help from Heaven, the organization's further growth will be towards spreading Rav Dror's pure teachings, educating the world in a Torah-based path, producing and providing the resources needed to do so, and in doing so, truly reuniting the world with their Father in Heaven.

◆ ◆ ◆

לעילוי נשמת
אהרן בן ישראל

L'iluy Nishmas
Aharon ben Yisrael

Cyndi Rand

Dedicated for Health of My Sister
Bethsaida Perez

Raul Martinez

Dedicated to My Grandmother of Blessed Memory

Jewl R. Mathis

Jacq Mathis

Dedicated to the Health and Divine Supervision of My Family and Grandchildren

May HaShem Watch Over You Forever

Donna Waters

Dedicated to the Souls of
Aurea Camoral Navarro
and
Armando Aquino Navarro

Arlene Bandond

Dedicated to the
Ostrava-Biala Rebbe
& Dr. Thomas Sharon

Blessings and Complete Success for
Michelle Jarboe, His Sons,
Friends and Loved Ones

Blessings and thanks to those
who supported this project:

David Elberg

Heuran Hoxha

Nelson Lane

Ilya Newman

Elizabeth Pride
Dedicated to Every Struggling Addict
May Your Life Be Made Whole By the Grace of Hashem

Robert Young
Blessed are the Peacemakers

Edward Zarrachi

Made in the USA
Monee, IL
27 October 2022

16668763R10095